THE KISS
of HEAVEN

"THIS BOOK *of the* LAW SHALL NOT DEPART
TATE *in* IT DAY *and* NIGHT, THAT YOU MAY
WRITTEN *in* IT. FOR THEN YOU WILL MAKE
WILL HAVE GOOD SUCCESS."

THE KISS

GOD'S FAVOR *to* EMPOWER

DARLENE

FROM YOUR MOUTH, BUT YOU SHALL MEDI-

OBSERVE *to* DO ACCORDING *to* ALL THAT IS

YOUR WAY PROSPEROUS, *and* THEN YOU

joshua 1:8 (nkjv)

# of HEAVEN

YOUR LIFE DREAM

ZSCHECH

BETHANYHOUSE

Minneapolis, Minnesota

The Kiss of Heaven
Copyright © 2003
Darlene Zschech

Cover design by office of Bill Chiaravalle, Sisters, Oregon
Interior design by Jennifer Parker

Manuscript developed in association with Cristine Bolley,
Wings Unlimited Editorial Services, P.O. Box 691532,
Tulsa, OK 74169–1532

Word meanings are taken from *Strong's Exhaustive Concordance* and *Vine's Expository Dictionary of Biblical Words* (Copyright © 1985, Thomas Nelson Publishers).

All song lyrics used by permission of Hillsong Publishing, Australia.

Photo credits: 35, 36 Tying the Knot Wedding Photography—Stephen and Jennifer Bebb:
91, 92 David Anderson.

Roman type is used within Scripture quotes to show author's emphasis.

Scripture credits at the end of the book are a continuation of the copyright page.

Published by Bethany House Publishers
11400 Hampshire Avenue South
Bloomington, Minnesota 55438
www.bethanyhouse.com

Bethany House Publishers is a Division of
Baker Book House Company, Grand Rapids, Michigan.

Printed in the United States of America

Library of Congress Cataloging-in-Publication Data

Zschech, Darlene.
    The kiss of heaven : God's favor to empower your life dream / by Darlene Zschech.
      p. cm.
    ISBN 0-7642-2780-7 (alk. paper)
    1. God—Worship and love. 2. Spirituality. 3. Christian life. I. Title.

BV4817.Z73   2003
248.4—dc21
                                        2003013794

To Amy, Chloe, and Zoe Jewel,
My three princesses.
Your future fuels my today.
You taught us to look for
Heaven's Exchange.
The greatest reward on earth
is the honor of being your mum.

♡ ♡ ♡

ENDORSEMENTS

Endorsements

"*The Kiss of Heaven* is worth reading just to know the preciousness of the story behind 'Shout to the Lord'—a song that has evoked praises to God across the face of our planet. It is the story of a remarkable composer and worship leader's life and growth in learning the marvels that proceed from finding God's favor, walking in it, and discovering with amazement the generosities heaven waits to bestow on any of us who will step forward with simplicity and sincerity into God's pathways—to following Jesus unto the highest purposes of the Father's benevolent intent for each of our lives."

DR. JACK W. HAYFORD
CHANCELLOR, THE KING'S COLLEGE AND SEMINARY

"God has used Darlene Zschech to touch the lives of millions of people around the world through her songs. As her success continues to grow as both an artist and songwriter, she has never stopped growing in Christ. Her commitment to spiritual and musical excellence continues to challenge and encourage me. I have always been impressed with something Darlene says during her concerts. Something like, 'The world system says if you're beautiful, talented, and special, you can be used. But in the kingdom of God, everyone is accepted and welcomed and beautiful in His eyes.' As you read *The Kiss of Heaven,* I pray that you will begin to see the wonderful plans God has for you and that you will have the courage to step into all that God has for you! What an exciting journey!"

DON MOEN
MUSICIAN, WORSHIP LEADER, AND
SINGER/SONGWRITER, "GOD WILL MAKE A WAY"

"Darlene's passionate pursuit of God's purpose has caused Him to breathe favor upon every area of her life. This is much more than a written book—it is a lived-out life. Darlene shares in a very practical, insightful way the simple yet profound principles of God that will liberate you to see the fulfillment of your dream through an abundance of heaven's favor."

NANCY ALCORN
PRESIDENT AND FOUNDER, MERCY MINISTRIES

"Darlene Zschech is well-known for leading and inspiring thousands of extravagant worshipers all over the world to touch heaven and change earth. Yet even though God has raised her up to have an international ministry platform, she remains ever humble and in awe of His grace and favor.

"In this book, Darlene describes the unfolding revelation of her personal journey with the Lord of her life and how her experience of His 'kiss' has impacted the course of her life.

"Instead of seeking to promote her own gift, Darlene discovered the powerful truth of seeking first the kingdom and sowing her life into building His church. Her insights will inspire you to pursue Him with your whole heart and, in doing so, live the life that you may have only dreamed about."

BRIAN HOUSTON
SENIOR PASTOR, HILLSONG CHURCH

ACKNOWLEDGMENTS

My magnificent husband, Mark, who continually inspires me to dream big . . . to live the greatest life together we could possibly imagine. Thank you for giving your life to help God's dream come to pass in so many others. I love that I'm God's chosen for you.

Patrick Judd, whose original vision for the need of this work brought the team together that made it happen. Thank you for your continued support and heart for the kingdom.

Miffy Swan, my faithful friend whose assistance with research and drafting of my notes kept the book moving to completion. Your position in life is inspiring. I'm honored to have you in my world.

Josh Bonett, thank you again for your heart, for seeing through the eyes of an artist, and for your whatever-it-takes attitude in serving the bigger picture.

Kristy Langford, Lisa Sylvester, Mel Hope, Tam Tickner, Simone Ridley, all the wonderful friends who do life with us, our worship and creative arts team, and the pastors and church family of Hillsong Church. We count it an honor and a joy to serve God alongside you. Especially to my pastor, Brian Houston, and to Pastor Robert Fergusson for your ever-inspiring teaching that continually frames my world. Thank you.

Eugene Petersen for *The Message* . . . thank you.

Bethany House editor, Steve Laube, whose excellence of heart brought clarity to the work.

Cris Bolley . . . for setting my pen in motion . . . and for allowing the dream in my heart to become reality.

To my wonderful Jesus . . .
    my desire is to live
        my life as an offering to You.

"And he [Jesus] said: 'I tell you the truth, unless you change and become like little children, you will never enter the kingdom of heaven.'

"Therefore, whoever humbles himself like this child is the greatest in the kingdom of heaven."

matthew 18:3-4

CONTENTS

Favor

- AN ACT *of* GRACIOUS KINDNESS

- AN ADVANTAGE *to the* BENEFIT
of SOMEONE *or* SOMETHING

- AN INCLINATION *to* APPROVE

- A FEELING *of* FAVORABLE REGARD

- TO PROMOTE OVER ANOTHER

Introduction

THE POWER OF FAVOR

I'm delighted that you have found yourself reading this book. I pray that your heart will be inspired and encouraged as you read through these pages filled with stories and truths designed to feed your soul, challenge your life, and just maybe paint for you a slightly different picture of what the favor of God looks like, sounds like, and was designed to accomplish in your life.

I believe beyond a shadow of a doubt that each one of us, no matter where you've come from or where you find yourself today, has been lovingly created and fashioned by our beautiful God and trusted, yes trusted, with this season in history. (What an overwhelming responsibility.) This fact should cause us to live purpose-driven lives—lives lived passionately, with an understanding that our time on earth was never given to us as a gift purely for ourselves, but that our lives should lift the lives of others.

If this all sounds a little surreal or if you've never had a personal encounter with Jesus Christ, then hang on with me through to the end of the book. The heartbeat of heaven is that you would know this wonderful Savior and that through life in Christ you will discover life *in Him;* living with freedom, purpose, and favor. At the end of the book is a prayer you can pray to make a commitment to Christ and His ways. How magnificent.

"Kiss of Heaven" . . . the word *kiss* is significant as it depicts intimacy and an exchange that happens only when you are up close. It's funny that so many people desire the fruit of God's favor (His kiss) but are unwilling to remain close to Him to do what He asks and to love and live by His Word. He so desires to be close to you and is just waiting for you to desire to be close to Him.

I was initially asked to write this book because so many people wanted to know how "Shout to the Lord," a song written by an Aussie girl, could become a favorite worship song around the world. Could it have been *favor*? Since the song was released in 1993, it has been recorded on more than fifty albums and translated into many languages, including Hungarian, Danish, French, Italian, Mandarin, Japanese, and Swedish. It has been played in church services, conventions, concerts, weddings, and even funerals. When first released, it was the fastest-moving song in the history of Christian Copyright License (CCLI), representing the popularity of all songs sung in churches. It has been sung in amazing places, such as the Vatican and the White House. Evander Holyfield was broadcast globally singing "Shout to the Lord" in his dressing room just before his world championship fight against Mike Tyson in 1997.

The "big story" behind this song is all about God's unmerited favor. I didn't sit down with the intention to write a song that would touch the nations. I am more surprised than anyone that this personal prayer has touched so many lives. In fact, the *big story* that has gripped my heart and become this book you hold in your hands today is about the amazing, incredible, overwhelming greatness of our loving God, who has shown and continues to show *great* grace to us all. He has given so much, each day is *kissed* by His grace. Our lives were designed by Him to carry favor—to serve the earth through the gifts He has given us. I see the songwriter John Newton penning those lyrics that sound so much like my life! "Amazing Grace, how sweet the sound, that saved a wretch like me!" My heart is so thankful to my loving God, who literally saved me.

I had been writing songs since I was a teenager, but I never really thought of myself as a songwriter. The day the words of "Shout" poured out of me was a day when I felt overwhelmed by life. It seemed like circumstances were smothering me, with no way out. In fact, life was just a grind . . . hard work with absolutely no "flow" connected to it.

I was desperate for God's peace when I opened my Bible to the Psalms. I read, "Sing to the Lord a new song; sing to the Lord, all the earth! Sing to the Lord, bless (affectionately praise) His name; show forth His salvation from day to day. Declare His glory among the nations, His marvelous works among all the peoples" (Psalm 96:1–3 AMP). My heart began to strengthen as I read the promise that God preserves the lives of His children; He delivers them out of the hand of the wicked. The Word says, "Light is sown for the [uncompromisingly] righteous and strewn along their pathway, and joy for the upright in heart [*the irrepressible joy which comes from consciousness of His favor and protection*]. Rejoice in the Lord, you [consistently] righteous (upright and in right standing with God), and give thanks at the remembrance of His holiness" (Psalm 97:11–12 AMP). As I continued reading this passage through Psalm 100, I could feel the crescendo of truth the psalmist must have known as he wrote these words:

> *Make a joyful noise to the Lord, all you lands!*
> *Serve the Lord with gladness!*
> *Come before His presence with singing!*

*Know (perceive, recognize, and understand with approval)
that the Lord is God!
It is He Who has made us, not we ourselves [and we are
His]!
We are His people and the sheep of His pasture.
Enter into His gates with thanksgiving
and bring a thank offering
and into His courts with praise!
Be thankful and say so to Him,
bless and affectionately praise His name!
For the Lord is good;
His mercy and loving-kindness are everlasting,
His faithfulness and truth endure to all generations.*
(Psalm 100 AMP)

After reading these magnificent words, I sat at my much-loved, untuned old piano that my parents had given me when I was five years old. Some of the keys didn't even play anymore, but I began to worship and play, praying and singing, and very quickly "Shout to the Lord" flowed from my heart. The entire song poured out in about twenty minutes. (I wish all songs were written that quickly!) I sang it over and over again, and it lifted me to a new height of faith. In that particularly hard season of my life, I simply expressed a genuine desire to praise, and soon my heart was lifted again. I continued to sing the song over the next few days. Eventually it occurred to me that this song might be a worship song we could sing at church. God blessed those words, *kissed* them with His favor, and chose to use them to set people free with the truth of His mercy and grace.

I felt uncomfortable about playing the song for our music ministers. My hands were sweaty, and I was just so nervous! I kept starting and stopping and apologizing for it before I even sang. The only way I could finally play for them was by making them turn around with their backs to me. I still smile as I remember how they patiently faced the wall as I sang for them that first time.

Everyone proclaimed the song majestic, but I honestly believed they were just being polite. Later when Pastor Brian Houston heard the song for the first time, he predicted it would be sung around the world. The rest is history—*His story*. It was God's favor on the song, and He did all the work required to share it worldwide.

Before the song had even been recorded on an album, I began receiving letters from people who were singing it in their churches. This was never the intention of the song. My heart's cry was to bring a sacrifice of praise, not to write melodies that would be shared by so many. God rescued me, as is His nature to do, and put an anthem of praise in my heart through His Word from the Psalms, and He carried that song to the world.

Whenever I reread this passage from the Psalms, I can still see the sea roaring and the mountains bowing down. I just offered my true love to the Lord, in awe of who He is, knowing He would *never* leave me. He will always provide a way of escape.

Favor—what does this word mean to you? I am sure God's definition of *favor* in our lives is far beyond what we would ever dare to imagine! *Favor* sounds quite intangible—reserved for a handful of special people. It is almost like a wish, a far-off dream, an ethereal ray of light. Maybe for you favor would look like having a home filled with family, buying a new car or house, or winning the lottery. Realistically, favor for my life will look different from favor for your life, because *you won't recognize a situation as favored unless it is of value to you.* This is the wonderful thing about our loving God, who wired each of us magnificently and uniquely to see His plans fulfilled on the earth.

I guarantee, when you have a healthy understanding of the grace and favor of God, it fills you with "irrepressible joy which comes from consciousness of His favor and protection" (Psalm 97:11 AMP)—an understanding and awareness of His beautiful nail-scarred hand on your life. I know from trial and error that loving God with your *whole* heart brings an incomparable sense of fulfillment. As you continue to read, I will share with you by way of testimony four keys: a fully devoted heart—devoted to His Word, devoted to His worship, devoted to His walk, and devoted to His work. These keys have helped unlock my heart to the too-beautiful-for-words love of God. Through loving Him, you too will find fulfillment and sense His smile as you live the God-dream for your life.

SENSE HIS SMILE. . .

the kiss of heaven

$\mathcal{O}ne$

THE KISS OF HEAVEN

The very first time I used the phrase "kiss of heaven" was just after the birth of our first daughter, Amy Jaye. I was scrambling to find a way to describe *knowing* that the supernatural has intervened to bring you to the place you are in today. I think my heart had asked to be a mother as long as I can remember. Years before we became pregnant, I collected baby things—even with the name *Amy* printed on them! I am so very thankful to my ever-patient husband for not dashing my hopes as I built my collection of baby items.

By the time Amy was on her way to us, I was *so* ready for my dream to come true. My fairy-tale picture of motherhood portrayed me lying in the hospital bed surrounded by ivory roses (my favorite flower), my hair and makeup perfect (just like the movies), holding my newborn beautifully swathed in a magnificent pink muslin wrap, and of course I was immediately back to my pre-pregnancy shape.

When I actually went into labor, I did my hair and makeup (as planned), put a pink ribbon in my hair (as planned), dressed as nicely as I could (considering my size), and off we went. Reality had not kicked in. I was a first-time mum with no clue as to what was in front of me. I hadn't yet really grasped the concept of why birthing babies is called *labor*. I took too long doing my makeup and made it to hospital too late for any pain relief. Somewhere in the haze of contractions I remember begging the doctor, "Kill me! PLEEEASE!!"

And then . . .
I gave birth to a divine answer to prayer,
pink and beautiful . . .
8 lb., 14 oz., Amy Jaye Zschech!

The photo of me holding Amy soon after birth does not look anything like my carefully planned portrait of motherhood! There I sat with my hospital gown half done up, my eye makeup smeared down to my cheekbones, baby hidden by the hugest hospital blanket ever. And the pink ribbon? It was around my neck!

However, by that afternoon I was severely bitten by the "baby-love bug." I was totally and utterly besotted by this "dream come true" lying in her little crib beside me. Out of my mouth, to my very tired husband, came the words, "The only way I can describe this is as though God himself has come and kissed me on the head. She is our very own 'kiss of heaven.'" (I tell A.J. all the time, "God kissed me on the head the day you were born." She rolls her eyes and just says, "Yeah, yeah, Mum. You've told me that a million times!")

I was totally and utterly besotted

by this "dream come true" lying

in her little crib beside me.

James 2:20 says, "Faith without works is dead" (NKJV). So it is with God's favor: You can't just cross your fingers, take no action, and hope for the best. But when diligence, obedience, and trust in God are combined with the supernatural hand of our Almighty God; well, there you have it—*the Kiss.*

In 2000 I wrote a song entitled "Kiss of Heaven" for an album called the *Mercy Project.* The words of this title are what come to me continually whenever I try to intelligibly describe that sense of *heaven touching earth*—when someone's life is totally and miraculously turned around through relationship with his or her Creator. It is the most appropriate way I can explain how He has transformed my life, giving me beauty for ashes, a garment of praise for the spirit of heaviness, the oil of joy for mourning. How beautiful is our God!

We all have dreams, aspirations, and goals we want to achieve—some grand, some noble, some small. In aspiring to achieve so many things, first and foremost, I *know* that to enjoy and to be aware of God's continual presence is one of life's greatest pleasures, and to give God our whole heart is His greatest delight. "For the eyes of the LORD range throughout the earth to strengthen those whose hearts are fully committed to him" (2 Chronicles 16:9).

His favor is lavished upon those whose hearts are completely His.

It is totally awe-inspiring to realize that God, the Creator of heaven and earth, is eagerly looking for people who believe in Him and have committed to loving Him completely. His grace is available to *all* who receive salvation; His favor is lavished upon those whose hearts are completely His. He is looking for wholly dedicated believers through whom He can shine. I always wanted to believe in my heart that He could shine through me, but it took a while for me to understand that it was even possible.

God is watching for someone to kiss with His favor even at this very moment. He watches—hoping to see our hands lifted up to love Him, serve Him, and receive His help so He can demonstrate His loving power through us to a love-starved planet. As I travel the continents of the world to lead praise and worship among God's people, I can almost feel the longing in God's own heart as He searches for individuals who will yield their entire confidence to Him. "For the eyes of the Lord search back and forth across the whole earth, looking for people whose hearts are perfect toward him, so that he can show his great power in helping them" (2 Chronicles 16:9 TLB).

To seek God's blessing in our lives is not a selfish ambition if we understand the reason that blessing is given. Favor is not designed so we can become hoarders of goodness, but it is given to those proven trustworthy, with open hands to receive and open hands to give. His undeserved grace and favor on the works of our hands give evidence to a lost world that He exists and is powerful to make His promises come alive for us. As we keep our eyes focused on the Lord and obey His direction for our daily lives, others will see the benefits of His favor on us, and they will be encouraged to also walk in His radiant presence. We are blessed to bless others!

So many Christians are missing the glorious benefits of God's continual presence. They enjoy brief moments of awareness of His presence, but sometimes the stories of their encounters with Him are many years old. Their faces radiate as they share their testimony of His rescue or provision that first drew them to Him, but then their countenance quickly dims as they speak of their current trials.

My deepest desire is to worship and love my God with all my heart, all my soul, and all my strength (Deuteronomy 6:5) and to inspire others into wholehearted *daily* lifestyle worship of our living God. The Father longs to rescue you every moment of every day. He wants your testimony of His mercy to be new each morning. He has new ideas to give us and new understanding to reveal to us. His matchless creativity is unending and largely unexplored, and He wants to demonstrate His magnificence to the world through the inspiring, God-filled lives of His people. Psalm 33:3 says, "Sing to him a new song; play skillfully, and shout for joy." The Word actually commands us to sing a new song and to shout, to make known, the goodness of our King.

Jesus taught that we are to ask God for daily bread, which is a beautiful picture of God's continual provision for our lives. He told His disciples,

> *Stop being perpetually uneasy (anxious and worried) about your life, what you shall eat or what you shall drink, and about your body, what you shall put on. Is not life greater [in quality] than food, and the body [far above and more excellent] than clothing?*
>
> *For the Gentiles (heathen) wish for and crave and dili-*

*gently seek all these things, and your heavenly Father well
knows that you need them all.*

*But seek (aim at and strive after) first of all His king-
dom, and His righteousness [His way of doing and being
right], and then all these things taken together will be given
you besides.* (Matthew 6:25, 32–33 AMP)

I love this Scripture. Again the Lord shows us where to
place our value while living this life. It's the wonderful reality again of serving Jesus—you are excited about life, filled
with passion and zeal, and continually realizing His
involvement in taking you to a point of fulfillment. You
seek God's righteousness, peace, and joy in the Holy Spirit,
and, just as promised, God is faithful to give you above and
beyond everything you need to achieve your sense of purpose on earth. Graced for life, and favored for living.

*The contrast between those who
seek God and those who seek
only His benefits is severe.*

The contrast between those who seek God and those
who seek only His benefits is severe. Many believers continually find themselves frustrated, I believe, because instead
of pursuing Him, they devote their energy to seeking a title,

recognition, and the appearance or trappings of success. I recently heard this kind of behavior described as living under "cheap grace"—devoid of an understanding of the price paid for us. It's halfhearted; it's hearing without listening, breathing without living.

The journey from halfhearted to wholehearted is one I know well. I had so many insecurities, wrong thinking, *and* vain ambitions (which I had carefully nurtured over the years!) that had to be quieted in me before I could even start to believe that God had a perfect plan to unfold for my life. Now I know it's called pride, but at the time, I didn't want to hear it! Even at a young age I sensed that God's plan was far greater than my own, and I earnestly prayed that God would somehow use me. But when I first started serving within the house of God, I didn't understand that He could use my unique experience and gifts to serve His calling on my life, that I had been lovingly crafted, just like you are, for divine purpose.

I tried so many ways to use my gift. I went anywhere there was an opportunity to sing. I was saved, I knew the Lord, but I was still trying to find my place. That sense of fulfillment seemed to continually elude me. I sang advertising jingles, and walked through just about any door that opened out of fear of missing out. I had no understanding of what it meant to know my life purpose and pursue it with all of my being.

It was easy to trust God with my spiritual life, and I

loved Him immensely. But I was very nervous about using all of my time and energy to serve my local church for fear of what that would involve. My deep sense of insecurity, inadequacy, intimidation, and all the other "in" words almost left me down for the count!

I didn't find it easy to trust God to use the natural abilities He had given to me. On a spiritual level, I loved God and loved to worship Him, but when it meant actually giving my time and energy to serve Him, well, that was a very, very different thing. My inner man and my outer man were at odds—the seen and the unseen did not meet at all!

My heart and my passion was music, but I tried to keep that interest separate from serving the Lord. Aren't we funny? I somehow never imagined that God would ask me to serve Him through what I loved to do. I thought somehow that was carnal, and I would be much more spiritual if I served doing something I hated to do!

I now understand that God is faithful to complete the good work He begins in us. He doesn't ask us to conform to the world or to each other. We are to serve one another with our own unique gifts. We are not asked to hide our true selves in order to fit in. He did not make *one* mistake when we were created.

The Song of Solomon 6:8–9 reveals God's delight over our individuality: "Sixty queens there may be, and eighty concubines, and virgins beyond number; *but my dove, my perfect one, is unique, the only daughter of her mother, the favorite of the one who bore her."* Understanding and truly knowing that God created each of us unique, different, and designed with purpose, allows my heart to trust, to "be still and know that [he is] God" (Psalm 46:10), to see His grace and His undeserved favor revealed over my life, allowing His dream to surface!

BUT BLESSED IS *the* MAN WHO TRUSTS *in the* LORD, WHOSE CONFIDENCE IS *in* HIM.

jeremiah 17:7

HIS FAVOR LASTS *a* LIFETIME.

psalm 30:5

jesus—the dream-maker

Two

JESUS — THE DREAM-MAKER

I t's surprising how many people have never been told that God has a magnificent, predestined plan for their lives. Many of those who have been told still doubt whether it could really be possible for them. Yet most feel a sense of destiny propelling them to develop certain skills and talents or to pursue specific opportunities that may bring that sense of wholeness.

The truth is that God does have a plan for each of us and has already equipped us with all the gifting we need to see that plan unfold. He plants a seed of that dream in our hearts before we are even old enough to feel it growing. Psalm 139:13–18 explains,

> *For you created my inmost being; you knit me together in my mother's womb. I praise you because I am fearfully*

and wonderfully made; your works are wonderful, I know that full well.

My frame was not hidden from you when I was made in the secret place. When I was woven together in the depths of the earth, your eyes saw my unformed body. All the days ordained for me were written in your book before one of them came to be.

How precious to me are your thoughts, O God! How vast is the sum of them! Were I to count them, they would outnumber the grains of sand. When I awake, I am still with you.

Mark and I are still completely overwhelmed by the path we are walking, our friends, our family, our church, and the new dreams God is birthing inside us! Looking back on our journey to date, we can see so clearly that He was working to demonstrate His power in a glorious way, and that has given us unshakeable faith for the dream that continues to grow in our hearts.

The Lord promises to work out everything for His own ends (see Proverbs 16:3–7). We know that if we commit our way, our plans, our thoughts, and our intents to Him, His favor moves in our behalf.

I remember one day we were driving to the beach and listening to a talkback program on the radio. I must mention here that Amy and Chloe cannot stand it when their dad listens to talkback radio! A girl rang up the talk-show host and was basically complaining about her day and her life—how hopeless life is for so many!

The radio host said, "Why is that?"

She answered, "My life goes to prove that the chaos theory is alive and well." It was a sad statement of fact from a young girl who was *so* disheartened and obviously feeling trapped on life's merry-go-round, wondering how she could get off!

The chaos theory proposes that life is simply on "automatic pilot," and that unorchestrated events just happen.

The Word says, "We are assured and know that [God being a partner in their labor], all things work together and are [fitting into a plan] for good to and for those *who love God and are called according to [His] design and purpose*" (Romans 8:28 AMP). Yet people all over the world are largely unaware of God's ability to work all things together for good, because they have not responded to His call and purpose for their lives. The world has taught them that their lives evolved from the chaos theory. If you buy into that lie, your life will seem so frustrating, empty, and unprotected.

Many reason that the earth "just happened" without

God. Through collisions of matter and then a lot of random accidents, our incredible solar system (with planets working in perfect, astronomical and meticulous, shimmering, divine beauty and harmony with each other) just worked itself out! The chaos theory proposes that life is simply on "automatic pilot," and that unorchestrated events just happen. If things are bad, well, so be it, and if they're good, don't get used to it.

In the first book of the Bible, Genesis, God's Word says that the earth began without form and was empty, with deep darkness. But with His great command and creativity, God organized the chaos and gave form to the heavens and the earth. He divided the seas, filled the oceans with sea creatures and the air with birds, and brought form and body out of nothingness. I find the world's chaos theory much more difficult to believe than the undeniable evidence of God's purposeful creativity. Throughout the Bible there are many seemingly random events that turned out to be a specific part of God's perfect plan, for a purpose much greater than merely for the individual to whom they happened.

The infant Moses was put into a basket and floated down the river "randomly" to where King Pharaoh's daughter found him and picked him up out of the water. This very king, who had planned to kill all the Hebrew boys, protected, loved, and provided for Moses, allowing his daughter to raise him as her own child until he was old enough to lead the people of Israel away from the king's bondage of slavery.

In a discussion about the need to pay taxes, Jesus told Peter to open the mouth of the first fish he caught and give the coin in its mouth to the tax collectors (Matthew 17:27). Was it another random event? Or is it evidence that our omnipotent (having unlimited power, able to do anything, all-powerful, almighty, invincible, supreme, unconquerable) Father has an awesome plan for His people?

By a miracle, God can suspend natural laws, if needed, to work out His plans on our behalf.

Many accounts are given in God's Word to show that He can use anything to achieve His purposes. He can use our failures as well as our triumphs to glorify His name in the earth. If you have made mistakes, welcome to humanity! That's why we need a Savior—that's why we need Jesus. His gift of salvation, His capacity to forgive and restore lives, is the power of the Cross.

By a miracle, God can suspend natural laws, if needed, to work out His plans on our behalf. He can bestow favor on us, as He did with Moses, so that even our enemies work to bring God's perfect plan into fruition for us. He prospers us for our own benefit and for the greater purpose of shining through our lives as a light of hope to a world that needs to put its trust in Him.

Most people, whether believers or non-believers, would admit to acknowledging some sense of destiny or purpose propelling them in life. The Word says, "He causes his sun to rise on the evil and the good, and sends rain on the righteous and the unrighteous" (Matthew 5:45). Even before we put our trust in Jesus, God is constantly working to bring about His perfect will for us, drawing humankind to himself.

God values us because we are adopted into His family, not because we offer our talents to serve Him. But even if we accept the fact that salvation is a free gift, it is sometimes difficult to give up the mindset that we must perform to keep His favor. His desire to bless us does not come through *doing for Him,* but through *devotion to Him.* I remained trapped in this disabling pattern of thought for years and found it difficult to accept that God loved me for who I am and not for what I do. I needed to accept that my salvation would never have to be earned and that my value was established in the heart of my God long before He trusted me with certain gifts.

For you created my inmost being;
    you knit me together in my mother's womb.
I praise you because I am fearfully and wonderfully made;
    your works are wonderful,
    I know that full well.
My frame was not hidden from you
    When I was made in the secret place.
When I was woven together in the depths of the earth,
    your eyes saws my unformed body.
All the days ordained for me
    were written in your book
    before one of them can to be.
        (Psalm 139:13–16)

God's Word is clear that His grace on us is undeserved. He extended His hand and offered the gift of salvation—there is no additional exchange required. We are to simply receive His grace with thanksgiving.

Understanding the righteousness of Christ…

and how He makes us RIGHT…

is quite breathtaking.

[Therefore, I do not treat God's gracious gift as something of minor importance and defeat its very purpose]; I do

not set aside and invalidate and frustrate and nullify the grace (unmerited favor) of God. For if justification (righteousness, acquittal from guilt) comes through [observing the ritual of] the Law, then Christ (the Messiah) died groundlessly and to no purpose and in vain.—His death was then wholly superfluous. (Galatians 2:21 AMP)

If you seek to be justified and declared righteous and to be given a right standing with God through the Law, you are brought to nothing and so separated (severed) from Christ. You have fallen away from grace—from God's gracious favor and unmerited blessing. (Galatians 5:4 AMP)

I love the way *The Message* Bible explains how God works through us, instead of our working for God. It says, *"May Jesus himself and God our Father, who reached out in love* and surprised you with gifts of unending help and confidence, *put a fresh heart in you, invigorate your work, enliven your speech"* (2 Thessalonians 2:16–17 THE MESSAGE). What an amazing Savior! Jesus himself will work on our behalf to make the dreams that He gives to us happen. The Lord will invigorate our work and enliven our speech so that His plans for us will succeed. But notice, He invigorates *our* work and enlivens *our* speech!

The parable in Matthew 25:14–30 illustrates the principle of how the Lord gives us something to use on His behalf to bring increase into His kingdom. In this story the master entrusted talents (of monetary value) to each of his servants (see verse 15). Likewise, God gives us talents (our

natural abilities and gifts) that can be invested to increase
His kingdom. Notice that the two servants who knew the
goodness of their master's heart were not afraid to take a
risk and invest their talents in something that would bring
increase. Consequently, they both doubled their investment
and were able to give back to their master twice the amount
they had been given. But the one who buried his talent
because he feared what the master would do if he lost it,
was called wicked, lazy, and idle. What talent he had been
given was taken away and put into the hands of a servant
who could use it for the master's "increase."

*We have a responsibility for the gifts
God has entrusted to us.*

We have a responsibility for the gifts God has entrusted
to us. What talents have you been given? Are they buried,
or are you using them? A gift to you, my friend, may look
like something you desire to have, but in reality, it is anything you are prepared to *give*!

In Exodus 36 we read about the people who labored to
build God's tabernacle. Every skilled person to whom the
Lord had given ability and skill was *willing* to come and
give and do the work, driven by their dream to build a
magnificent temple that would be worthy of housing His

glory. God is calling you to use your gifts and develop your skills to serve the world in some way. His plans and purpose for you outweigh anything you could ever imagine. He has made His intentions clear for all of us saying,

> *"For I know the plans I have for you,"* declares the LORD, *"plans to prosper you and not to harm you, plans to give you hope and a future. Then you will call upon me and come and pray to me, and I will listen to you. You will seek me and find me when you seek me with all your heart"* (Jeremiah 29:11–13).

I pray as you read on that you will be encouraged to examine the calling in your heart, consider the gifts you have been given, and exchange your fears for faith in God's ability to preserve and prepare you for the dream He has seeded within you.

> *With this in mind, we constantly pray for you, that our God may count you worthy of his calling, and that by his power he may fulfill every good purpose of yours and every act prompted by your faith. We pray this so that the name of our Lord Jesus may be glorified in you, and you in him, according to the grace of our God and the Lord Jesus Christ.* (2 Thessalonians 1:11–12)

The works of your hands become an act of worship when the attitude of your heart is to demonstrate to others the glory of His goodness in your life. May we all hear Jesus say to us, "Well done, good and faithful servant! You have been faithful with a few things; I will put you in charge of many things. Come and share your master's happiness!" (Matthew 25:21).

For *a* DREAM COMES *through*

MUCH ACTIVITY...

ecclesiastes 5:3 (nkjv)

what is the desire of
your heart?

$\mathcal{T}hree$

WHAT IS THE DESIRE OF YOUR HEART?

G od has breathed a dream into every individual, regardless of whether or not they are devoted to Him. He calls each of us to participate in His great plan for the world. Romans 1:19–20 says, "Since what may be known about God is plain to them, because God has made it plain to them. For since the creation of the world God's invisible qualities—his eternal power and divine nature—have been clearly seen, being understood from what has been made, so that men are without excuse."

Because God works all things together according to His purpose, He places deep within each of us an incredible desire to know Him. Once the fullness of God is known to you, your passions are redirected and your pursuits are driven by a different set of values. *Desire* is a powerful emotion and needs the direction of a healthy heart to bring about healthy results.

Too often, we find ourselves trying to gratify our passions, and we all know too well that life without Christ is futile—like climbing a mountain and never quite getting to the top. Never satisfied, our empty hearts are ready to grasp or swallow any delusional teaching or scheme that may be cleverly disguised as truth. But true believers are of a different seed. They drink from the fountain of life, their faces pointing upward toward the Son. They live in favor, even in difficult times—hence the invocation, "Let your face shine upon me."

Because God works all things together according to His purpose, He places deep within each of us an incredible desire to know Him.

When we delight in God, He promises to give us the desires and secret petitions of our hearts. The thought of living to delight the heart of God has grown in me as I have grown in Him. Psalm 37:3–4 reassures us that God will bring those desires to pass as we commit our way to Him.

God has given and entrusted gifts to every single person on earth, but there are so many factors that can distract us from ever realizing the potential or the hope we have inside. Yet that God-breathed dream inside of you has the power to lift you out of the mindset that you could never fulfill your dreams. Imagine if we had a glimpse of our true capacity!

The apostle Paul explained this purpose and calling in his letter to the church saying,

> *And he made known to us the mystery of his will according to his good pleasure, which he purposed in Christ, to be put into effect when the times will have reached their fulfillment—to bring all things in heaven and on earth together under one head, even Christ.*
>
> *In him* we were also chosen, having been predestined according to the plan of him who works out everything in conformity with the purpose of his will, *in order that* we, who were the first to hope in Christ, might be for the praise of his glory. *And you also were included in Christ when you heard the word of truth, the gospel of your salvation. Having believed, you were marked in him with a seal, the promised Holy Spirit, who is a deposit guaranteeing our inheritance until the redemption of those who are God's possession—to the praise of his glory.* (Ephesians 1:9–14)

The complexity and intricacies of human beings are so wonderfully rich in life, in purpose, in function, in creativity, in reproduction, and in balance, designed in perfection according to God's blueprint. Yet ever since Eden, we have struggled, blinded by the master deceiver as he has tried to question, manipulate, confuse, undermine, and devalue the very worth and reason for God's pride and joy. Being made in God's image, His creative nature is continually seen through the lives of His children.

I once watched Sting in concert (he was absolutely incredible!). *So* much "gift" for one human being! Thoughts raced through my head, *My goodness, Sting, you are like King David, full of psalms, melodies, and music, and you sing as if you don't even know that His hand is upon you. You are so close to the heart of God. You are a master poet, full of love; and your capabilities are not because of your own natural abilities—you have tapped into the source of your Creator.* I could *see* God's dream-seed at work in him; I could *see* God's call on his life.

The fulfillment of a God-dream always takes great courage, for they are always *so* much bigger than ourselves. Bill Gates changed the way our world communicates, but his bigger dream is to wipe out polio. His dream has a greater purpose than himself. Where would that dream come from, if not from God?

Martin Luther King had a God-dream that ignited harmony and freedom for our world. His dream was empowered and fueled by his consuming passion to see people in bondage set free. Sounds like a God-dream to me.

Mother Teresa was born into destiny in God's perfect timeline within eternity, born to fulfill His purpose. This tiny little lady, with sharp focus and a heart full of love and compassion for people, has left a legacy and challenge to all who dare to trust Jesus with their lives. Not a popular dream, but oh, *such* a God-dream.

Oprah Winfrey is a woman who has herself been touched by grace. Whether you love her approach or not, she devotes *so* much time, resources, and energy to seeing people's lives lifted. Could this be the seed of a God-dream?

Nancy Alcorn (a little dynamo and a dear friend) saw injustice done one too many times and founded Mercy Ministries, a program dedicated to seeing young women's lives restored. A big dream, one woman, great courage—an amazing God.

Nelson Mandela—a brave man with such a powerful conviction that he denied his own freedom to ensure the freedom of countless thousands.

You could all add your own stories of people you know who live to lift the lives of others. We could fill every page with great examples of so many others, known and unknown, who have lived with great courage to see their hearts' dreams come to pass.

We are created in God's image, and our lives were meant to be a visual demonstration of His awesome glory and goodness. When we turn away from God and go our own way, we walk away from our purpose and our only hope of true fulfillment. There are many brilliant people, both alive and deceased, who were entrusted with things from heaven, but they never understood what they had and why. There are way too many stories of people who held brilliance in their hands, but who chose to take themselves out because they couldn't live under the weight of such greatness. We can find success apart from God, but we can't find eternal fulfillment without Him.

Ask yourself the questions under "What Is Your Dream?" Write down your answers. It quite possibly will give you a great insight into the life you've been favored to live.

Humanity is hungry for God's presence in their everyday lives. In order for people to see God's glory and His goodness, we must be willing to allow His potential within each of us to be unveiled. When people see God at work through the fulfillment of our goals and dreams, they just may trust Him for dreams of their own.

I HAVE *a* DREAM. IT IS *a* DREAM DEEPLY ROOTED *in the* AMERICAN DREAM. I HAVE *a* DREAM *that* ONE DAY OUR NATION WILL RISE UP *and* LIVE OUT *the* TRUE MEANING *of* ITS CREED—"WE HOLD THESE TRUTHS *to be* SELF EVIDENT *that* ALL MEN ARE CREATED EQUAL." I HAVE *a* DREAM THAT *on the* RED HILLS *of* GEORGIA, *the* SONS *of* FORMER SLAVES *and the* SONS *of* FORMER SLAVE OWNERS WILL BE ABLE *to* SIT *at the* TABLE *of* BROTHERHOOD. I HAVE *a* DREAM *that* ONE DAY, EVEN *the* STATE *of* MISSISSIPPI, *a* STATE SWELTERING *from the* HEAT *of* INJUSTICE, SWELTERING *from the* HEAT *of* OPPRESSION, WILL BE TRANSFORMED *into an* OASIS *of* FREEDOM *and* JUSTICE. I HAVE *a* DREAM *that* MY FOUR LITTLE CHILDREN WILL ONE DAY LIVE *in a* NATION WHERE THEY WILL NOT BE JUDGED *by the* COLOR *of* THEIR SKIN BUT *by the* CONTENT *of* THEIR CHARACTER. I HAVE *a* DREAM TODAY. . . .

martin luther king, jr.

What Is Your Dream?

WHAT IS *in* YOUR HEART *to* DO?

WHAT ARE *the* SECRET PETITIONS
of YOUR HEART?

WHAT DO YOU WISH YOU COULD BE?

WHAT COULD YOU DO, *or* BE PART OF,
to BLESS SOMEONE ELSE'S WORLD?

WHAT ARE YOU GOOD AT?

WHAT WOULD YOU DO IF TIME *and*
RESOURCES WERE UNLIMITED *to* YOU?

WHAT DO YOU FIND EASY?

WHAT MOVES YOU?

WHAT IDEA ARE YOU HESITANT *to* SPEAK OUT
LOUD BECAUSE IT IS SO BIG *and* SO DARING?

Humanity is hungry for God's presence in their everyday lives.

When we know God's Word, we understand that He "is able to do immeasurably more than all we ask or imagine, according to his power that is at work within us" (Ephesians 3:20). In the next verse He promises this to each and every generation, forever and ever!

Yet when it comes to acting on our God-given dream, we so often lack courage and confidence, and we refuse to see ourselves as God sees us. This not only limits us, but it can paralyze us so that we simply settle with our lot in life. We watch others run with their dreams, but we are unable to step out in faith and see our own heart's desires become reality.

The starting point to see a God-given dream fulfilled is simply to step out, to make a start, to *start where you are!* All *greatness* starts somewhere, usually in some little "backside of the desert" in less-than-grand surroundings, trusting God's favor to bring it to pass. If you lack the faith, goodness, knowledge, self-control, perseverance, godliness, brotherly kindness, and love needed to make your life grow to maturity, then you are in great company! Ask God to give you wisdom, for His power gives us everything we need for life.

Write the Vision

Early in our married life, Mark and I decided to write down our goals—short-term and long-term, some lifetime aspirations. We asked God to direct our efforts, just as the Word says, "A man's heart plans his way, but the LORD directs his steps" (Proverbs 16:9 NKJV). In fact, every new year while on holiday we take time to go over our goals and dreams, see how far we have come, and look at things we may need to reevaluate.

Jeremiah 10:23 says, "I know, O LORD, that a man's life is not his own; it is not for man to direct his steps." Writing down our dreams helps us to pay close attention to what God is inspiring us to do and fulfills the instruction of Proverbs 4:20–23, "My son, *pay attention* to what I say; listen closely *to my words. Do not let them out of your sight,* keep them within your heart; for they are life to those who find them and health to a man's whole body. Above all else, guard your heart, for it is the wellspring of life." In fact, I always sense that whenever I commit the desires in my heart to paper, I literally set them in motion. Cool!

Your dream may become clear to you like a visitation from God, but it may also come as a small, gentle whisper in your spirit or as a recurring desire within you that only you can sense. Some people waste years waiting for a great knock on the door, fanfare, lights in the sky, a visitation from angels, or the voice of a prophet saying, "God has told me to tell you. . . ." But all Mark and I ever had was a longing in our hearts and the Word of God, which encourages us continually to be faithful, to be a servant, and to bless the Lord at all times. Sounds so easy!!

My position as a worship pastor did not begin with a dream to lead worship. Far from it. I simply began my journey in loving Him, serving in the house of God, making coffees, running errands, being available, doing whatever needed to be done, spending time getting to know Him, and learning to welcome His presence in my life.

Once you sense the dream at work in your heart, write it down. Keep track of your desires by writing out the vision of what you want to see happen in your life. Be really brave in writing down what you would like to see fulfilled. This will help to bring clarity and to recognize God's hand and favor on your future as you bravely begin to walk in it. Habakkuk 2:2–3 says,

> *And the Lord answered me and said,* Write the vision *and engrave it so plainly upon tablets that every one who passes may be able to read [it easily and quickly] as he hastens by.*
>
> *For the vision is yet for an appointed time and* it hastens to the end [fulfillment]; *it will not deceive or disappoint. Though it tarry, wait [earnestly] for it; because* it will surely come; *it will not be behindhand on its appointed day.* (AMP)

Don't be afraid to talk to people you trust and love

about your vision for your life. Your dream will be tested in time. And if you are worried about whether it is God's will, just go back to the foundational question again: Will this desire bless others? Will it help build the kingdom of God? Is it in line with God's desire for my life? God's plan for your life will not contradict His Word—don't *ever* let anyone tell you otherwise!

It's not enough to have a dream without a plan of action. To raise my daughters the way I dream requires a personal commitment from me that involves time, energy, more energy, and all the other things that go hand in hand with parenting.

Whatever it is you truly value, that is where you'll place your time, energy, attention, finances, love, and devotion. In fact, you'll see quickly the things you value by looking at where you spend your time, energy, and dollars when you don't have to! True success in life is costly. We can be *so* quick to come up with all the reasons why we can't follow the call of God in our lives, blaming so many other factors for what may be our own inability to persevere, and quick to tear down others when their lives are starting to have influence.

Acting on my dream is up to me. I can't blame the devil if my dream of creating a great home life doesn't happen just because I spend my time sleeping the day away or being too busy to bother. Creating a great marriage doesn't happen just because you dream about it. It's a *decision;* you work hard at it because it is valuable to you.

I have dreams for many areas of life, and sometimes it's hard to juggle my time. In this journey of life, Mark and I *so* desire to always be a blessing to our church. Because I feel that this is a desire that stems from heaven itself, it doesn't conflict with my desire to be a great homemaker and to build a *strong* family!

God has graced us with all the hours we need each day to fulfill all that is required of us to do—time for family, time for work, time for friendship, and time for rest. There is a lovely promise in Mark 10:29–30:

> *"I tell you the truth," Jesus replied, "no one who has left home or brothers or sisters or mother or father or children or fields for me and the gospel will fail to receive a hundred times as much in this present age (homes, brothers, sisters, mothers, children and fields—and with them, persecutions) and in the age to come, eternal life."*

Make Plans to Achieve Your Dream

In 1999, while traveling in the United States, I stumbled across a little old antique bookshop filled with "preloved" treasures. Right at the back, lying sideways against the wall, was a timber sign hand-painted with the words "Faith, Family, and Friends." My heart leapt, because these are the three things in life that I value the most. So for the next three weeks we carted that sign around the U.S., until it finally made it to our home. We now have those words engraved over our mantelpiece to constantly remind us to cherish and take time to build the foundations of our lives to a place of strength and depth.

Jesus came, lived, and died for you and me. Heaven aches and God exists for humankind. If people cease to matter to us, we cease to function in the way we were created to function. We were designed to connect. Connecting is life! In connecting with God we find true life, and as we connect with others, life in Christ is shared, nourished, challenged, and enhanced.

Having somewhere to live is a house;
having someone to love is a family.

A rescued POW, when asked what he had learned through his hell-on-earth experience, replied, "To love Jesus more, and to love and value my family." God created this beautiful institution called family—the stretching, loving, often hard-work component of close relationship. Eugene Peterson said, "Without costly love, there can be no connection, no future, and no success together. If connection is life, then loneliness is the ultimate horror. God himself sets the lonely, the widow, the orphan, the misfit—in family." Having somewhere to live is a house; having someone to love is a family.

If this is an area that represents hurt and disappointment for you and you desire to be connected to family, then *friendship* just might be where you find it. This wonderful, heaven-kissed body called the church, when operating in the supernatural, will quickly find friends turning into family.

Seek First Righteousness, Peace, and Joy

Let your focus be to know the King and to seek His kingdom first. When you do this, Jesus said that *all these things* (our desires) would be added to our lives (see Matthew 6:33). "For the kingdom of God is not a matter of eating and drinking, but of righteousness, peace and joy in the Holy Spirit, because anyone who serves Christ in this way is pleasing to God and approved by men" (Romans

14:17–18). In 1 Corinthians 4:20–21 we read, "The kingdom of God is not a matter of talk but of power. What do you prefer? Shall I come to you with a whip, or in love and with a gentle spirit?"

The Word is clear that if we seek God's way of living, He will give us the desires and petitions of our hearts. Jesus desires to give us the abundant life—a glimpse of heaven on earth.

The Beatitudes (Matthew 5:2–12)

This is what he taught them:

God blesses those who realize their need for Him, for the kingdom of heaven is given to them.

God blesses those who mourn, for they will be comforted.

God blesses those who are gentle and lowly, for the whole earth will belong to them.

God blesses those who are hungry and thirsty for justice, for they will receive it in full.

God blesses those who are merciful, for they will be shown mercy.

God blesses those whose hearts are pure, for they will see God.

God blesses those who work for peace, for they will be called the children of God.

God blesses those who are persecuted because they live for God, for the kingdom of heaven is theirs.

God blesses you when you are mocked and persecuted and lied about because you are my followers. Be happy about it! Be very glad! For a great reward awaits you in heaven. And remember, the ancient prophets were persecuted too (author's paraphrase).

"NEVER LET ANYTHING *so* FILL YOU
     with SORROW *as to* MAKE YOU FORGET
     the JOY *of* CHRIST RISEN...."

mother teresa

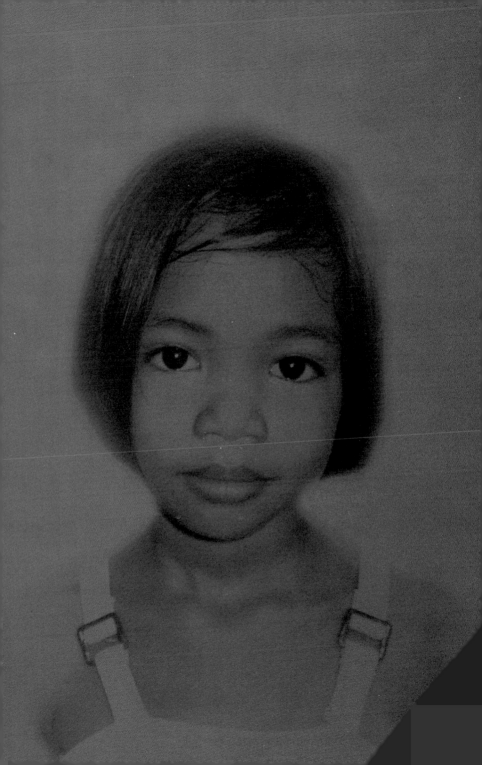

the dream-stealer
favor in unfavorable times

Four

THE DREAM-STEALER

I can guarantee that as you start to rise up and step out, taking initiative, with that little spark of confidence starting to glow within you, you *will* face opposition. Whether it is old ways of thinking, a lack of support from those around you, or the devil himself coming at you . . . you will need to allow the pressure to build your strength, to give you some backbone, rather than let it defeat you.

Mark and I had spoken a lot about a specific dream for something that was very dear to our hearts. This dream had been ignited when we were dating! We had a desire to start a ministry in our nation to broken young women, but weren't really sure—well, that's such an understatement . . . we had *absolutely no idea* what that would actually look like. Then in 1999 a day of destiny, which I'll never forget, began to unfold before us when we met Nancy Alcorn (this lovely champion woman I mentioned before), founder of Mercy Ministries in America. She had been working with troubled youth since 1973, starting her first home for unwed mothers in 1983. Since then hundreds of unwed mothers and troubled young women have found unconditional love, hope, restoration, and healing through this much-needed ministry. Meanwhile, God had begun to stir up Nancy's heart to pray for Australia.

After meeting with Nancy, we knew in our hearts that God had connected us for the specific purpose of starting up this very timely ministry in Australia. Nancy's mission was like seeing in real time a picture we'd only imagined before. God is patient—not rushed by our eagerness. He cannot be bribed or cajoled! He fulfills the work that He starts in us according to His timing. When His timing is in place, He moves quickly and makes up for the time we have had to wait on Him.

By the time I began writing this book, we had purchased our first home for Mercy Ministries in Sydney. We wanted a home in a beautiful part of Sydney, where the young women could come free of charge and sense the awesome ability of God to make a bright future for them in spite of a dark beginning. He has provided a property near our church that seems tailor-made for our mission. It has many bedrooms, game rooms, and beautiful gardens surrounding the property on several acres of land in one of the most desired neighborhoods of Sydney. Although initially the community was against having this residential property used for Mercy Ministries, prayer and the support of outstanding key community leaders helped us to gain approval from the mayor and members of his council.

God was already working on

the fulfillment of the dream

when He planted the idea of it in our hearts

so many years ago.

Little Do We Know

God was already working on the fulfillment of the dream when He planted the idea of it in our hearts so many years ago and was weaving this dream throughout the lives of many others. Jenni Fairbairn, a native of Sydney, was the first international graduate of Mercy Ministries of America. She had sought for so long to receive help in our country, but found none, and through sheer desperation she made the trip to the U.S. to receive help! She was battling with drugs, alcohol, and severe anorexia, weighing only forty-three kilograms (about ninety-five pounds). She shares in her own words:

Life was always very confusing for me, and I spent much of my time wondering who I was and who I was meant to be. I seriously thought that God had made a mistake when He made Jenni Fairbairn. Little did I know at this time what great things He had planned for me.

I walked through the door of Mercy Ministries desperate, broken, and with very little hope. I needed a miracle, and I knew deep down that God was the only One who could help me. I had searched everywhere. The government programs were able to take me if I had twelve to eighteen months to wait, but I knew I didn't have that much time.

The love and acceptance I received at Mercy were like nothing I had ever experienced before. I couldn't believe these people genuinely cared for me and didn't expect anything in return. I was blown away by their unconditional love.

Within a year at Mercy Ministries, Jenni was able to walk with her head held high, no longer ashamed of her past and now excited about her future. God had a dream-seed at work in Jenni. The enemy, who comes to kill, steal, and destroy, would have loved to not only steal Jen's dream, but her very life! But there we find it again, the Kiss of Heaven. Our God is *awesome*!

Jenni began working with Mark and me to open Mercy Australia. Mercy Australia is the realization of a God-given dream that has come true. That dream keeps growing as we continue to pray for God's timing to open many homes throughout Australia and New Zealand, and we have already opened our second home in Queensland.

Don't listen to the wrong voices during your time of waiting on God.

We now understand that we must wait for God's appointed time. We were faithful with what God put in our hands, but when we started we had no resources, no offices, no staff . . . seems like the perfect ingredients to attract the heavenly favor to me . . . to see this God-dream become a reality. If you don't have the qualifications, the background, the education, or even at times, the support of those close to you, well . . . all I can say is, then at least you can be sure that as this seed in you starts to grow and flourish, *all* the glory goes to God! Serving God is costly—there's no doubt about it—but the price is nothing compared to the great joy you find in His service. It is not a joy that is dependent on circumstance—*nothing* can steal the joy of a devoted believer. Many people run from their dreams when they learn it will cost patience, perseverance, and endurance. They don't want to pay the cost the dream will require.

Don't listen to the wrong voices during your time of

waiting on God. Instead, resist the dream-stealer by surrounding yourself with godly people who will lift your faith and not people who just give you advice from their own logic. Seeing your way through to the completion of a God-given dream takes great courage.

There are countless thousands of people who have led the way for us, courageously pursuing godly, noble missions. For example, Marilyn Hickey is a woman whom I so admire, who has the courage to pursue a dream from God. Seemingly born in the wrong generation, when women were discouraged from ministry, she broke loose from the natural limitations she was presented with, and has lived her life, living her dream to cover the earth with the Word of God, her life's passion. Her dream-seed began by working hard, late at night, while her family slept, making recordings of the Word of God for those who needed to hear. No woman before her was doing anything like that; they weren't supposed to. But she had a dream in her heart.

When Marilyn's daughter Sarah had her first baby, Sarah called me to tell me her awesome news. I asked her, "Where's your mum? Is she doing well?" Sarah said, "She's climbing over the walls of Sudan, covering the earth with the Word." Marilyn was in her late sixties at the time, but her dream-seed had pulled her out of herself, because her dream is greater than herself. *So inspiring!*

Favor in Unfavorable Times

The word *favor* almost depicts a "perfect" life—living in the sunshine of promise twenty-four hours a day, never a trouble, nothing to overcome, no mountains to climb, not a problem in the world. Well, that, my friend, is reserved for heaven. You must realize that if that is your concept of how life on earth should be and anything that doesn't measure up to this picture leaves you disappointed, then your moments of real joy will be so fleeting that *nothing* will ever satisfy you.

In the middle of 2002 Mark and I, together with our family and a wonderful team from Compassion Australia, took a long-awaited trip to Bangkok and Chiang Mai, Thailand, and Manila, Philippines, to visit two of our sponsored children. We were looking forward so much to meeting them and their families and to seeing where they lived and the kind of difference child sponsorship truly made. We were also nervous about what we would find in some of the slums that we were going to visit, wondering how the experience would affect our girls, and asking God for wisdom in bringing change to such harsh circumstances.

Yes, we saw incredible hardship, we wept at the appalling conditions families had to endure, and we were overwhelmed by feelings of helplessness at the sheer enormity of heartache. But we also found a depth of human spirit and kindness that was too brilliant to ignore, and we discovered a fresh revelation of God's favor in the worst of situations, yet again revealing the heart of our Father toward humanity.

Job never abandoned or walked away from his dedication to his God.

In the Word, wherever Jesus was revealed, there were answers; wherever He was known, there was provision, even if it came moment by moment. Wherever the reality of Christ was acknowledged, there was hope. Here were all these children with nothing, absolutely nothing of any earthly value, yet they had a glimmer in their eyes and an innocent, simple, deep understanding that they were loved beyond measure by their heavenly Father. I was so inspired to see the love of Christ at work and the determination of these magnificent human beings to seek His face and His will for their lives, to be obedient, and to trust Him with their future.

There's an incredible Scripture in Job 10:12 that says, "You have granted me life and favor, and Your care has preserved my spirit" (NKJV). In the midst of Job's hell-on-earth experience, even though he occasionally found himself arguing *with* God, Job never abandoned or walked away from his dedication *to* his God. In the first chapter of Job, even after his livelihood, his riches, and his beloved children were taken from him, the very first thing he did was fall to the ground in worship. Job's true devotion was obvious in abundance, and just as obvious in adversity. The most beautiful realization Job had in the midst of it all was the awareness of the kindness and *care* of his Lord.

Just as the Psalms instruct us to do, we need to *selah* (wait, pause, think about this moment). In the time it takes you to become disappointed or disheartened about the situation in which you find yourself, you can choose to take the same moment and look for God's divine favor, to *lift up your head*. Again, it's a choice. We do not deserve grace and favor, but we do attract it. He will *never* let you down. Things may pan out differently than you expected, but God himself, who promises to never leave you or forsake you, will come through. That's the funny thing about faith. It is what our lives hang from; it is so real. The Word even describes it as substance, evidence yet unseen (see Hebrews 11:1 NKJV). Trust is invisible to the human eye, but oh so real to the human spirit.

Another wonderful experience we encountered on that same trip was a worship service put on by the children of Compassion. Again, many parentless children, living in such basic, sometimes squalid, conditions, came together to bring an offering of worship to their Lord and Savior for all He has done and is doing in their lives. They sang song after song to exalt Him for who He is, never complaining, blessed in their simple human condition of living in the joy of salvation. I could sense the heart of God being blessed— *divine*!

Never again will I complain about getting up early when my tiredness is mainly due to the long hours required to *live a blessed life*! My woes were completely put into perspective, and again our motives were challenged and refined as we were led into the depths of truthful worship by these living legends—true twenty-first-century heroes!

Jesus is the difference, my friends. He works. In the third world, where the inadequacies of the most prosperous nations on earth are allowing millions to live in extreme poverty, the Word still works. When you are faced with life or death situations, guess what—the Word of God works. It is alive; it is revolutionary; and if you are truly at the end of yourself, the Word of God cannot lie and will always sustain your spirit. That is what favor looks like.

Dreams were often used by God in the Old Testament as a means of divine revelation. In Genesis 37 a great story begins to unfold about a young man named Joseph. He was a shepherd (what is it about shepherds and greatness?) who was described as being favored by his father because he was born to him in his old age. Joseph was a dreamer, and the dream described in verses 5–7 must have captivated him, because he shared it with his brothers, much to their indignation at his so-called arrogance and overconfidence.

You would think Joseph would have learned that he was not going to get the yearned-for support from his brothers. But no, he told them of his next dream, making them even more angry (see Genesis 37:9). I guess the content would have totally derailed them, as it was an example of how they would soon, along with the stars in the sky, be found bowing down to him. You know the story. Eventually they were sick of his seemingly haughty attitude and plotted to kill him. *Extreme!* His eldest brother intervened and had him put in a waterless well. From that moment, even to the outsider, it seemed like Joseph's life was over.

Things went from bad to worse—from the well to being sold into slavery (see Genesis 37:18–24). God continued to make a way where there was no way. Eventually Joseph was taken to the house of Potiphar (a palace official). There Joseph again found favor. Genesis 39:2–6 states that the Lord was with Joseph, and he prospered, living under the "kiss of heaven." As soon as it was evident in Potiphar's eyes that Joseph had the divine favor of God and that the Lord gave him success in everything he did, Potiphar put him in charge of everything he owned. The story continues like the movie *Groundhog Day*. Joseph finds himself again unjustly thrown into prison. But our tenacious Joseph had a dream, and even in prison the Lord was with him and granted him kindness and favor (see Genesis 39:21).

Eventually Joseph became ruler over Egypt, and just as

in the dream God revealed to him earlier, all of the people, including his brothers, came to bow before him. The loveliest statement is made when Joseph names his second son. He calls him Ephraim, saying, "It is because God has made me fruitful in the land of my suffering" (Genesis 41:52)—another great example of divine favor.

If you are serving God, loving Him in all you do, I encourage you to be strong; do not lose heart. Just as He did for Joseph, God works on our behalf for His plan to unfold. *No man, no wicked schemes* can come in the way of the Almighty!

God doesn't cause our hopes and dreams to die. We must encourage each other to ignore the devil's lies and hold on to the fact that God has breathed life into us and has given us dreams to achieve and to enjoy. Too many people have suffered from a life that has been messed up by the dream-stealer, and now they simply survive with no passion for life.

You don't want to get to the end of your life and hear "done" instead of "well done." Resist the enemy, who tries to steal our dreams. We must stand firm, even when there is no natural ability to stand. When life is hard, when we've lost a battle to the dream-stealer, we must not concede the war. We must use our faith and trust that God will give us the desires of our heart just as His Word promises. God's dreams are too precious to lay aside.

You don't want to get to the end of your life and hear "done" instead of "well done."

When we continue to trust God in moments that require faith to do so, we become strong. This kind of faithfulness reaches the very heart of God, and when personal disappointment results in worship, even when all seems dark around us, His open arms are there to comfort and strengthen. As I mentioned in *Extravagant Worship,* when I miscarried our much-loved little unborn child, God turned the incident that the dream-stealer used against me into a greater passion and conviction to worship God. That will never be stolen from me. I have a confidence that dreams will sprout from the seeds He has planted in all who sacrifice praise to Him.

Never Let Go of a Dream From God

Even though my parents continually spoke greatness into me and were an example of loving parents, the dream-stealer, with a glimpse into my potential, was hard at work to destroy me. I scrambled through my teenage years believing the worst about myself—believing I was fat and ugly, believing I needed to work harder to be loved more, to please, or to be accepted. I felt I was the reason for divorce in my family. It's a familiar story for too many young people.

Now I know it was the devil, the dream-stealer, who came to steal the future that God had placed in my young heart. He works especially hard on young people or on people with new dreams in their hearts so that he can dash all hope and kill a dream-seed in its tender beginnings. He took my baby before I even had a chance to fight for it. He steals—that's his personality—he's a thief.

God-dreams will always find opposition, even before you realize that your amazing idea may be more than a whimsical thought. How many times has a great idea come to you and then *instantly* you thought, *Ah, wouldn't that be great, but I could never. . . ?* When you hear the words *"I could never . . ."* know the enemy is planning your defeat rather than your victory, snuffing out a dream in its infancy.

When Jesus was born, the enemy of God put the desire in Herod to search for Him and have Him killed. Before

Moses was born, this same dream-stealer made Pharaoh decree that all baby boys were to be killed. The devil recognizes a God-dream long before we do.

In 1 Samuel we read that Satan tried to snuff out David's call to be God's chosen king over Israel. David was the least likely candidate to become the king—at least in the eyes of everyone else. When Samuel came to anoint one of the sons of Jesse to take Saul's place as ruler over God's people, David's own father didn't even think he deserved to be mentioned as one of his sons. That's how "the least" David was. Most of us believe we at least deserve to be mentioned as a member of our family! I believe the Enemy's plan was to kill God's dream for David in its infancy. David was the least of the least, but when God chose David, He told the prophet Samuel, "The LORD does not look at the things man looks at. Man looks at the outward appearance, but the LORD looks at the heart" (1 Samuel 16:7).

Let God Breathe Life Into Your Dream

You know a dream is from God when you can let go of it, but it won't let go of you. I am so thankful that God is outstandingly generous, and my dreams are fulfilled because of His grace to breathe life into the seeds of desire in my heart.

God breathed life into Adam; He breathed life into creation; and He wants to breathe life into the life that has been given to you. The life that God breathes is His supernatural presence to bring His favor and abundance into our natural life. It is the power to defeat the dream-stealer.

The supernatural life is being aware of the presence of God in all you do.

Jesus said that He came to bring us *life,* not death, and life to the *full.* He explained, "The thief cometh not, but for to steal, and to kill, and to destroy: I am come that they might have life [*zoe*], and that they might have it more abundantly" (John 10:10 KJV). The word *abundant* is from a Greek word *perissos* (per-is-soś), which means "superabundant in quantity" or "superior in quality," by implication, "excessive." In and through Christ, we have access to a life that is exceeding, abundantly above, more advantageous, very highly, beyond measure, more, superfluous, vehemently full of God's goodness. That's awesome!

You can live your whole life doing what is natural: get up in the morning, go to work, come home at the end of the day, go to sleep, and get up again the next day, only to do it all over again—that's a natural life. But the supernatural life is being aware of the presence of God in all you do. The supernatural life happens when you let God breathe His life into yours. Jesus is the dimension to our natural, everyday life that causes us to do the supernatural things that demonstrate the glory of His presence in our lives.

Even though your day may present you with events that could cause anger, the supernatural presence of God's life in you empowers you to respond with forgiveness. When someone does something to hurt you, your natural response might be bitterness. But that feeling can be supernaturally replaced by empathy and concern for the would-be offender. Supernatural joy replaces natural grief; mercy replaces retribution; and there is life where there would have been death.

Let me give you some dictionary descriptions of *grace:* a disposition of kindness and compassion, free and unmerited favor or beneficence of God, a state of sanctification by God, divine love and protection bestowed freely on people. Let's then compare those descriptions to *favor:* an act of gracious kindness, a feeling of favorable regard, considered as the favorite, bestow a privilege upon. There are only two Hebrew words in the Old Testament that are translated into the English word *grace,* and they both flow from the root word *chânan,* which is the same word used for *favor,* meaning to bend or stoop in kindness to an inferior; to beseech, to grant, to show mercy, to make supplication. *Strong's Concordance* gives only one English word—*favor*—

as a translation for the Greek word *charis,* which means graciousness of manner or act, especially the divine influence upon the heart—acceptable, benefit, favor, gift, gracious, joy, liberality, pleasure.

To try to separate the words *grace* and *favor* seems almost impossible. *Grace* is used to talk about our position in life, while *favor* is used much more frequently to talk about our mission. Grace to live and favor to move. I guess that's why both are inherently critical to being alive and being effective, "for in him we live and move and have our being" (Acts 17:28).

The word *grace* is most commonly used to express the concept of kindness toward someone totally undeserving. That's why it is described as the "unmerited favor of God." Grace is not merely the one act of kindness leading us toward salvation, but it is the factor that allows us the strength to maintain a powerful Christian life. Favor, in comparison, is not used often in the New Testament, but when it is, it is most often used in reference to someone doing good and then finding favor, and there is a supernatural element to it that is outside our control.

This is the full life that we need to let God breathe into us and into our dreams. I challenge you to inhale the very breath of God that causes natural things to fall away and the supernatural presence of God to fill your response to life. His life in us brings His favor—His abundant life. When the dream-stealer threatens the hope in your heart, run into the arms of the Dream-Giver. The only weapon Satan has against us is the lie that our dreams cannot come to pass. The dream-stealer is easy to defeat. The Bible says, "Submit yourselves, then, to God. Resist the devil, and he will flee from you" (James 4:7).

Be honest with God and tell Him when you feel overwhelmed. As you desire to serve Him in truth, adoring Him for being strong when you are weak, He will lift you up and carry you to a place of supernatural grace that won't just be a dream anymore. God will cause your dreams to become the reality of an abundant life in Him.

CHRIST IS *the* ONE THROUGH WHOM
GOD CREATED EVERYTHING
in HEAVEN AND EARTH.
HE MADE *the* THINGS WE SEE
and the THINGS WE CAN'T SEE—
KINGS, KINGDOMS,
RULERS, *and* AUTHORITIES.
EVERYTHING HAS BEEN CREATED
through HIM *and for* HIM.
HE EXISTED BEFORE EVERYTHING
ELSE BEGAN, *and* HE HOLDS
ALL CREATION TOGETHER.

colossians 1:16-17 (nlt)

the heaven exchange

$\mathcal{F}ive$

THE HEAVEN EXCHANGE

If you choose to see them, life is filled with glimpses of heaven's exchange in your world. These moments of trying to see life through God's eyes, to capture and remember His amazing faithfulness, have become anchors to hold me in place when new storms may come to rage against me.

One of these anchors of hope came to me when my father was dying of cancer. I was visiting him after what turned out to be his last operation, and he was about six weeks from passing away. He had a huge hole in his stomach that was not healing. I had become disillusioned. I wasn't angry with God, but I had a lot of questions to which I couldn't work out answers. My dad was so dear to me for many reasons, and it was through him that I really came to know Christ. I couldn't understand *why* Dad was not getting better. My dad, his friends, and his family all believed and waited for a miracle. He had been faithful to the Lord, and *I* felt he deserved a miracle!

As I sat near Dad one day, I talked to him about my questioning heart. I said, "Dad, I don't understand why you are suffering, because from what I read in God's Word—about our future and our hope—well, this isn't part of it. We really need a miracle."

I'll never forget the magnificent words my beloved father spoke to me from his hospital bed that day in late November 1990. Even though his body was ravaged by cancer, he looked at me with his beautiful smiling eyes and then said to me point blank, "My darling, I already *have* my miracle."

I looked at him in disbelief (thinking the pain-killers had gone to his head!). "I already have my miracle," Dad said again. "I know Jesus; I have salvation, and that is enough—that is enough for me."

In the natural, it was as though death had already visited, but Dad was still living under the favor of God. He could see heaven's exchange even though I could not. Dad's passion for God's viewpoint really tore my heart and challenged my life perspective, initiating a major mindset shift in my thinking. I now consider the confession of my mouth as I walk through life's trials, and I endeavor to trade my own perspective for heaven's perspective. Despite our circumstances, God promises to look on us with favor and keep His covenants with us. He promises to walk with us and keep us as His own (see Leviticus 26:9–12).

My dad saw that Jesus is the greatest miracle of all, and being able to comprehend His point of view is a great, great gift. Dad didn't need a healing miracle to feel fulfilled; his friendship with Jesus was the fulfillment of his life's purpose.

Learning to be a praiser is definitely a decision that we need to make every single day.

My father was a praiser! He saw life from God's viewpoint. He saw the best, and he had an ability to change his surroundings and influence those around him by confessing with his mouth the praise that was in his heart. Learning to be a praiser is definitely a decision that we need to make every single day. To praise God in the midst of threatening circumstances is a powerful principle of sacrifice that pleases Him. Praise is an atmosphere-changing principle, and *if* we can make it a way of life, praise has the ability to open up doors of possibility before us.

On December 8, 1990, my dear friend and father went home to be with his Jesus. Death held *no sting*. Dad's praising heart and uncompromising faith never wavered, and he danced on home to glory.

When you know grief so overwhelming that you feel you will drown in the depths of emotion, this is when you need to choose to worship the King—there at your lowest point. This is where the sweet presence of God will wash over you, and our Father will breathe His breath into your life, allowing you to rise again and find His grace and favor to go on.

When you feel your world is in complete darkness, choose to praise Him in the midst of it. God's glorious light will invade the situation, and the reality is that dark and light cannot coexist. An explosion of praise chases the darkness away, and again His kiss—the reality of why we need a Savior is revealed.

These are examples of what I call the *heaven exchange,* when God literally exchanges our weaknesses for His strength, our brokenness for His wholeness. He tells us, "My grace is sufficient for you, for my power is made perfect in weakness" (2 Corinthians 12:9).

When you stand and choose to rejoice in the face of opposition, you are literally using the spiritual warfare weapons Paul describes in 2 Corinthians 10:4: "The weapons we fight with are not the weapons of the world. On the contrary, they have divine power to demolish strongholds." Psalm 66:3 says, "So great is your power that your enemies cringe before you."

Moments of contentment must be connected to heaven in some way, because true happiness is a snapshot of God's grace being demonstrated to us. I know great people who enjoy moments of satisfaction and success, yet do not lead *fulfilled* lives. You can live a full life without it being a full, filled life.

> *You can live a full life*
>
> *without it being a full, filled life.*

God's dream for you is first *salvation,* to bless you with His fellowship and to bless others through the intimate friendship He has with you. These exchanges are available every day if we choose to see them.

Sometimes God offers heaven exchanges that we find difficult to trade, even when we want what He is giving to us. I remember such an exchange when God said to me that I would never have to perform for Him. It took a long time for me to see this truth from His perspective. Only when I understood all that Jesus did to win God's love toward me was I able to accept that I could never do more to deserve God's grace than Jesus had already done.

There are two ways to look at the daily challenges we face. One view is through the darkened eyes of hopelessness; the other is through the Tree of Life, with our face toward Him, seeing God working to exchange our current conflicts with His merciful glory. I have learned to focus on heaven's exchange by giving God all my cares and learning to do what David did in Psalm 4. In exchange, He gives me confidence to continue unafraid.

> *I will both lie down in peace, and sleep; for you alone, O* LORD, *make me dwell in safety.* (Psalm 4:8 NKJV)

The "evening psalm," as we have affectionately come to know Psalm 4, is perfectly titled. David's words in verse 4 are quoted in Ephesians 4:26–27: "'In your anger do not sin': Do not let the sun go down while you are still angry." In your life, don't give the devil a foothold by submitting to every whim of emotion that tries to rule you. David had surely come to the great realization that when he was outraged or his emotions were about to overtake him, wisdom shouted, "Wait!"

Selah. Take a moment to pause, think, and quiet your soul within you. Sounds like a yielded vessel to me. Sounds like self-control. Psalm 4:5 sums up this decision-making process quite bluntly: "Offer right sacrifices and trust in the LORD." Most decisions you make on a day-to-day basis to walk in the way of righteousness will require you to say no when you want to say yes. They will require you to close your mouth and say nothing when you feel you have much to say, or they will require you to give more than you know you have. Again we hear those words, "Trust in the Lord." Our Lord has already orchestrated His grace and favor for us, but it is up to us to implement it.

Heaven Exchanges Stress for His Glory

Several years ago Mark and I were sowing our time into services at our home church while struggling to make ends meet through sales in our motorcycle shop. I was the vocal director at the church, which required many hours of my time, and I also helped in our business by selling motorcycle parts over the phone. (I would just like to add here that I was not the greatest at this job, but I now know all about gaskets and oil filters!) Whenever I was able, I sang jingles (sessions, backing vocals, radio and TV ads), all the while working to balance my time to be Mum to our beautiful daughters.

I had made a commitment to give God everything I had, but eventually I thought, *Okay, I promised to give God my life, but now look where I am!* I was feeling worn out. I'd worked myself into a deep hole.

I have learned to love two words: *perseverance* and *patience* (maybe *love* is too strong a word!). In finding the heaven exchange, we must realize that we are never magically rescued in an instant from our troubles, but we are supernaturally made aware in an instant of His goodness, His favor, His timing, and His commitment to building our lives. How incredible it is that in that difficult and frustrating time in my life the song "Shout to the Lord" was birthed. The heaven exchange.

On another day in that same season of my life, when I was already very tired and frustrated, I opened the mail and found another bill for an overdraft. I thought, *I just can't go on another day. I can't do this anymore! God, what happened to your promise? I just can't believe this is happening to us.* You know the line: overworked and underpaid!

I have learned to love two words:

perseverance and patience.

Well, my thoughts of despair and tears of self-pity were interrupted by the sound of my daughters' laughter coming from the bedroom. Our little Chloe was nearly one year old, and Amy was almost four, and now their giggles sounded like they were into some grand mischief. I dashed into the room to see what the girls were into that seemed so funny to them. I will never forget the picture of their delight that day. There they were, my beautiful girls, totally undressed, happily jumping on the bed. Perhaps the fact that I had pulled the sheets off the bed to wash them caused the girls to see the bare mattress as an inviting playground. Each of them had a bottle of talcum powder that they were shaking as they jumped. Sunbeams were streaming through the window, giving the dusted, fragrant air a sense of ethereal wonder. I will never forget the picture of those two tiny, naked bodies, giggling in the sun-filled and talcum-powdered cloud. I walked into the room and just started laughing.

When God gives us a heaven exchange,
we are reminded of the true values of life.

Once again, God beautifully exchanged my view of our circumstances for His when I saw my happy babies playing carefree in the sunlight! It was such a lush picture of "casting your cares on Him!" They were *oblivious* to all of my grown-up worries. They just loved being alive, loving each other, and *loving* making a mess!

I sat on the floor beside the bed and laughed with my cherished daughters. Something in my heart whispered, *Everything is going to be okay.* I sensed heaven's smile. Just seconds before I had been distraught, thinking that favor was starting to feel like hell on earth, not heaven on earth! Then thirty seconds later, my dancing daughters had turned my heart around. God was seeing my life in a much more beautiful light that day than I had understood at that time.

When God gives us a heaven exchange, we are reminded of the true values of life. I am confident that God offers heaven exchanges to everyone who will choose to see them.

The Anchor of Hope

The following passage summarizes the anchor of hope that was given to Abraham, which has been passed on to us as heirs of his promise. We are to hold on to this hope when threatened by life's concerns. Our inheritance reads,

> *Blessing I certainly will bless you and multiplying I will multiply you. And so it was that he [Abraham], having waited long and endured patiently, realized and obtained [in the birth of Isaac as a pledge of what was to come] what God had promised him.*
>
> *Men indeed swear by a greater [than themselves], and with them in all disputes the oath taken for confirmation is final [ending strife]. Accordingly God also, in His desire to show more convincingly and beyond doubt, to those who were to inherit the promise, the unchangeableness of His purpose and plan, intervened (mediated) with an oath. This was so that by two unchangeable things [His promise and His oath], in which it is impossible for God ever to prove false or deceive us,* we who have fled [to Him] for refuge might have mighty indwelling strength and strong encouragement to grasp and hold fast the hope appointed for us and set before [us]. [Now] we have this [hope] as a sure and steadfast anchor of the soul—*it cannot slip and it cannot break down under whoever steps out upon it*—[a hope] that reaches farther and enters into [the very certainty of the Presence] within the veil, where Jesus has entered in for us [in advance], *a Forerunner having become a High Priest forever after the order [with the rank] of Melchizedek.* (Hebrews 6:14–20 AMP)

God's promise and oath are our hope, and this hope is

an anchor for the soul, firm and secure. If we give God everything, including our cares, He will work everything together to complete His plan for us.

Earlier this year I was having some serious voice problems. My body just did *not* want to sing. I would open up my mouth, and nothing beautiful would come out. It was *so* frustrating—I cannot begin to tell you. Well, it was the same time that President Bush had announced that war with Iraq was inevitable. There was fear all over the news. The frightening and heartbreaking state of the world was brought into the light again.

One morning after taking the girls to school, I grabbed a few moments at the piano. (Not the old untuned one; this one is beautiful and was given to me by a precious girl friend.) I just said to God, *My hope is not in my ability to sing for you; my trust is not in America's ability to win a war; my hope, my Father, is in your name.*

Here is part of the song that came from another heaven exchange.

"My Hope"

My hope is in the name of the Lord
Where my help comes from
You're my strength, my song
My trust is in the name of the Lord
And I will sing Your praise
You are faithful.

© 2002 Darlene Zschech/Hillsong Publishing

"IF *a* MAN IS CALLED *to* BE *a* STREETSWEEPER,
HE SHOULD SWEEP STREETS
EVEN *as* MICHELANGELO PAINTED,
or BEETHOVEN COMPOSED MUSIC,
or SHAKESPEARE WROTE POETRY.
HE SHOULD SWEEP STREETS SO WELL
THAT ALL *the* HOST *of* HEAVEN *and* EARTH
WILL PAUSE *to* SAY,
HERE LIVED *a* GREAT STREETSWEEPER
WHO DID HIS JOB WELL."

martin luther king, jr.

a fully devoted heart

A FULLY DEVOTED HEART

What does a fully devoted heart look like? It certainly doesn't look like religion, and it certainly doesn't look like a life of rules and regulations. We get a glimpse into a devoted heart when He gives us a new heart through salvation. Psalm 34:22 records a beautiful promise: "The Lord redeems the lives of His servants, and none of those who take refuge and trust in Him shall be condemned or held guilty" (AMP).

Salvation through Christ gives us a new life, free from the past, full of promise for today. A new heart is put within the core of our being, full of new motivation, a new value system, a new beginning, and a Savior to direct our steps. Salvation literally saves us. Anyone who has been physically rescued from imminent death always seems to report, one way or another, that they now live life with fresh perspective. What a gift!

When we devote our whole heart to God, we are never the same again. We are moved from a position of spiritual darkness to one of glorious light. God said of His people, "I will give them a heart to know me, that I am the LORD. They will be my people, and I will be their God, for they will return to me *with all their heart*." Just before this He said, "My eyes will watch over them for their good, and I will bring them back to this land. I will build them up and not tear them down; I will plant them and not uproot them" (Jeremiah 24:7, 6).

When we devote our whole heart to God,

we are never the same again.

A heart that treasures its Savior finds a wellspring of life that is impossible to ignore. As you delight in the King you will find yourself flourishing in hard times, singing in the midst of barrenness, smiling at the core of adversity, giving when there is nothing left to give, dancing when your limbs ache, loving when your heart is broken, and standing strong when going to bed seems like a better option!

Delight yourself also in the Lord, and He will give you the desires and secret petitions of your heart. Commit your way to the Lord—roll and repose [each care of] your road on Him; trust (lean on, rely on and be confident) also in Him, and He will bring it to pass. (Psalm 37:4–5 AMP)

The dreams within you need to be watered by His truth and warmed by the light of His presence in order for that seed to germinate, grow roots, and eventually bloom into something so beautiful and so brilliant that all who look upon the fruit of our lives will see God's unmerited kindness and power. God is both the Dream-Giver and the One who fulfills the dream He plants within us. "For it is God who works in you to will and to act according to his good purpose" (Philippians 2:13). When fully mature, the fruit of this seed will bring something far greater than success—it will reap an abundant harvest of fulfilling joy. That seed contains the answer to the frequently asked question, "How can I make my life meaningful?"

Psalm 1:3 continues to bring us simple answers. "He is like a tree planted by streams of water, which yields its fruit in season and whose leaf does not wither. Whatever he does prospers." There is nothing less palatable than fruit picked before its time. Pick fruit off a tree before it's ripe, and what does it taste like? It's either bitter or bland—it is either acrid or it has no taste, no flavor. If you take heed to this Scripture and run from sin, run from secrecy, run from bad habits, run from those things that align you with everything that does not represent the hand of God on your life, then, in season (which means in God's due time, when you are ready), the fruit of your life will be sweet and will flavor everything with which it comes into contact.

When you try to do your thing
and your dream, but not in God's time,
there is no flow to it.

When you are trying to pick fruit that's not ripe, it's hard to get it off the tree. It's the same way in life. You also have to strive and struggle when you try to operate out of God's time. When you try to do your thing and your dream, but not in God's time, there is no flow to it. But when it is in season, it's just like when you pick an orange off a tree that is ripe—it almost falls off; it is heavy, because it is full of juice; you can smell it before you cut it open. It is beautiful, and the juice is dripping everywhere. You put it in your mouth, and it is *so* good! That is what fruit in season is like, and when your season in life is right, there will be such an ease to it. It won't be bitter or tasteless. Often people who have gone out before their due season leave a trail of bitter, disillusioned people behind them. That is *not* the will of God.

Let go and let your whole heart embrace our God of wonders, for He will astound you again and again if you'll only let Him. When God-given dreams are achieved in His people, His glory (His amazing power, goodness, and kindness) is manifested in the earth and unbelievers are drawn to

His unmerited love. Your life has destiny written all over it. Love God with your whole heart, refill your life with faith through His Word, revitalize yourself with His friendship through worship, refuel yourself with His favor through your everyday walk, and then *watch out* as the windows of heaven begin to shine on all He has called you to do.

Be Wholly Devoted to the Lord

When I began writing this book, I was expecting our third daughter, Zoe Jewel. One day Mark, Amy, and Chloe went with me to the doctor to see an ultrasound of the little body growing rapidly within me. We were all a little nervous, because the last time we had done this, the results were devastating. It was thrilling for all of us to hear Zoe's tiny heart beating with new life! You could not wipe the smiles from our faces!

Later while at lunch with a friend, I shared the excitement I felt over not only hearing Zoe's heartbeat, but seeing it on the screen, pumping away in the perfect rhythm of life! It seemed that God was prompting me to explore more deeply how loving Him with our *whole* heart, with all chambers beating for Him, was relevant to His pleasure in us and to our own fulfillment in life. God said in His Word, "I will give you a new heart and put a new spirit in you; I will remove from you your heart of stone and give you a heart of flesh. And I will put my Spirit in you and move you to follow my decrees and be careful to keep my laws" (Ezekiel 36:26–27).

So I began researching the internal workings of the heart. Quite simply, the heart works as two pumps (stay with me here). Half of the heart pumps deoxygenated blood into the lungs, where the blood is reenergized (filled with oxygen again). The other half of the heart pumps oxygenated blood from the lungs out to the rest of the body.

I can see the parallel of how grace works like the muscle of our spiritual heart to pull our tired thoughts and human frailties back into the promises of God's Word, increasing our desire to worship Him in truth, where our thoughts are reenergized with His presence. The other half of our spiritual heart pumps this zealous faith into our daily walk with Him, anointing us with His favor for all He has purposed for us to do in order to carry life to the world.

Jesus said, "I am come that they might have life, and that they might have it more abundantly" (John 10:10 KJV). If you have trusted your life to Jesus, then you know how different life is since God gave you a new heart capable of pumping His life (the life of the Father himself) into your thoughts and out through your actions. But listen, dear friends, you must guard your heart. In Jeremiah 17:9 we are warned that "the heart is deceitful above all things."

Just as we must exercise to enhance our physical endurance, so we must walk in faith to strengthen our spiritual hearts.

In 2 Thessalonians 2:17 we read, "Comfort and encourage your hearts and strengthen them—make them steadfast and keep them unswerving—in every good work and word" (AMP). Unlike our natural hearts, which *automatically* circulate new life back into the whole body, we must exercise our spiritual hearts with faith to keep them strong. Just as we must exercise to enhance our physical endurance, so we must walk in faith to strengthen our spiritual hearts, for faith without works is dead.

Once my doctor put me on a treadmill for an endurance test to calculate the strength of my heart. It was brutal! But when the test was over and the results were strong, I felt awesome! Likewise, God allows our faith to be tested so that from a position of strength we can walk out what we truly believe.

God doesn't test us for His benefit—He does it for ours. "The Lord disciplines those he loves, and he punishes everyone he accepts as a son" (Hebrews 12:6). The test isn't for God to see; He knows us to the core. But each test of faith makes our hearts a little stronger, growing in maturity and wisdom, strength to strength, able to negotiate well the God-sized life that resides in us. "Blessed is the man who perseveres under trial, because when he has stood the test, he will receive the crown of life that God has promised to those who love him" (James 1:12).

Hebrews 5 addresses believers who have become sluggish in achieving spiritual insight, saying that they ought to be teaching others God's principles, but they are still inexperienced and unskilled in *purpose, thought, and action* concerning conforming to God's divine will (see v. 13 AMP). They are like babes, still requiring the milk of the Word instead of meat: "But solid food is for the mature, who by constant use have trained themselves to distinguish good from evil" (Hebrews 5:14). It is constant application of the Word of God in our daily lives that allows us to walk in the reality of our dreams. *The Amplified Bible* says it this way: "But solid food is for full-grown men, for those whose senses and mental faculties are trained *by practice* to discriminate and distinguish between what is morally good and noble and what is evil and contrary either to divine or human law." And the King James Version says strong meat belongs to "those who by *reason of use have their senses exercised* to discern both good and evil."

Halfhearted believers hear the Word of God, but never put it into practice, and then they wonder why they find themselves living in the land of frustration. *Been there, done that!* We're called to be doers of the Word and not hearers only.

Dare to be someone who

takes God's promises literally

and serves Him wholeheartedly

by living in His truth every day.

Don't be someone who chooses to serve God halfheartedly. Dare to be someone who takes God's promises literally and serves Him wholeheartedly by living in His truth every day, allowing it to transform you and then spreading this truth to others. That is the abundant life Jesus died to give you.

Be Wholly Available and Yielded to God

God delights in using ordinary people with devoted hearts to do extraordinary things and see the promises in His Word fulfilled. "He guards the lives of his faithful ones" (Psalm 97:10). It is beautiful to see how He bestows favor over the faithful ones. They can be talented and amazing, but that is not what ultimately blesses God's heart or what prompts Him to bless them.

I have seen this time and time again through our worship team. Talent is important, but it is not what ultimately brings lasting impact. I've seen many talented people come and go, often stirring up trouble as they huff and puff, trying to get themselves noticed. I know it sounds harsh, but to be honest, my heart through this book is to save your having to learn some of these life lessons the hard way. There is divine favor that comes through walking and persevering in something passionately and faithfully over a long time, not allowing your dream to be deterred by setbacks and obstacles. Just get good at trusting God and serving others.

Although many may try, you cannot separate His name from the word *blessing,* even if it makes you uncomfortable, because it is in His magnificent nature—part of the fabric of the Trinity. When we understand how much we have received through grace, we are humbled in God's presence. But in humbling ourselves before Him, He lifts us up again. God opposes the proud, but He gives grace to the humble (see 1 Peter 5:5–11). He will lift up the humble in due time. God bestows grace to restore us, and grace is the power that makes us strong, firm, and steadfast so that our hearts will please Him. Loving God with our whole heart is an invitation to cast our anxiety on Him because He cares so much. As I've heard it said, "Jesus would rather die than live without you."

Don't Despise the Day of Small Beginnings

When Mark and I first moved to Sydney, the first apartment we had was over a doctor's office, and we had to share the bathroom with his patients! It wasn't so bad, but one time we had a friend and his family stay at our flat when we were out of town. We forgot to tell him about the arrangement we had with the doctor about the bathroom. (Small detail!) When our friend finished his shower the next day, he opened the door to find a patient waiting her turn to come in. There he stood—wearing only a towel! We laugh about it now, but he didn't think it was so funny at the time.

Our goal was not to raise a family in a doctor's surgery . . . but in trusting God with your whole heart, the journey often looks a little different to what your ideal "faith brochure" looks like. He has always provided the way for His plans to come about. The key is to live in continual thankfulness for all that He does.

Devote your whole heart to Him . . . keep it with all diligence . . . for out of it spring the issues of life!

"WHAT DOES *the* FAVOR
of GOD LOOK LIKE?
THE GRACE *of* GOD, APPLIED DAILY,
OVER *a* LIFETIME."

mark zschech

devoted to his word

Seven

DEVOTED TO HIS WORD

"orget not my law or teaching, but let your heart keep
my commandments" (Proverbs 3:1 AMP). Most
Christians are familiar with the passage from Prov-
erbs 3:5–6, promising that God will bless us if we trust in
Him. But the verses before and after these famous words
are critical to direct us through a straight and plain path to
God's promise. Consider carefully the full passage from
Proverbs:

> *My son,* forget not *my law or teaching, but* let your
> heart keep my commandments;
> *For length of days, and years of* a life [worth living],
> and tranquility *[inward and outward and continuing
> through old age till death], these shall they add to you.*
> *Let not* mercy *and* kindness *[shutting out all hatred
> and selfishness], and* truth *[shutting out all deliberate*

*hypocrisy or falsehood] forsake you. Bind them about your
neck;* write them *upon the* tablet of your heart;

So shall you find favor, *good understanding and high
esteem in the sight [or judgment] of God and man.*

Lean on, trust *and* be confident *in the* LORD *with* all
your heart and mind, *and do not rely on your own insight
or understanding.*

*In all your ways know, recognize and acknowledge
Him, and He will direct and make straight and plain your
paths.* (Proverbs 3:1–6 AMP)

God's Word is our source of life. We will find favor,
understanding, and high esteem with both God and other
people if God's Word is alive in our hearts. I look at these
Scriptures very practically. If you are not great at showing
mercy, kindness, and truth to those in your world, then ask
God to teach you and train you. Be accountable to someone who will challenge you when your behavior is not in
line with the Word. These are *so* worth pursuing, for they
are part of the character of Christ and promise great favor
on your life.

The Gift of Peace

As your knowledge of God grows, so grows your peace.
I have noticed in my own walk with God that the more I
know Him, the more I find myself yielded to Him. Both

the written Word (His *logos*) and His spoken word (His *rhema*) fill us with peace. The Bible is jam-packed full of promises, direction, and principles for your life, and if you are listening, God is speaking to you all the time through reading His Word and directly to your heart through His still, small voice within you. Mind you, sometimes this seemingly small voice will seem *very* loud when God is trying to get your attention!

There have been *many* times, when I have glanced at a stranger, a family, mother and child—and something in me says, *Go and speak to them, spark up a conversation!* I think, *yes . . .* then I think, *no . . . don't be so crazy . . .* etc., etc., until this stirring within me has almost been audible—GO . . . SPEAK . . . NOW!

Every time I have obeyed the sweet voice of the Holy Spirit within me, I have had the opportunity to start a new friendship, or invite people to church, or just show kindness. You can be praying and praying for God to open doors to use you, yet miss countless opportunities right in front of you every single day.

God's Word is life to us;

it is as important as the air we breathe.

Jesus said, "Man shall not live by bread alone, but by every word that proceeds from the mouth of God" (Matthew 4:4 NKJV). God's Word is life to us; it is as important as the air we breathe. If we don't know what God has said in His Word, and if we never take time to be still and listen to Him, how can we have faith in His promises? And without faith it is impossible to please God (see Hebrews 11:6).

When the disciples asked Jesus to teach them how to pray, one of the things He told them to ask for was daily bread (see Matthew 6:11). I *love* fresh bread—that incredible smell and the soft white texture. Mmmm, there's nothing quite like it! It's the same with our spiritual life—we will never be satisfied living off yesterday's or someone else's revelation. I've said this many times before, but the pathway from you to God's throne should be a well-worn one.

By listening for Him to direct us throughout the decisions we face each day and by reading the Word of God to confirm His voice, we grow in the knowledge of who He is and who we are in Christ. When we understand our place in Christ, we will never want to settle for anything less than His perfect will and purpose for our lives.

Peace comes when we're not striving, not trying to earn His love and promise, because God's favor is our enabling energy to serve Him, or you will sense it wash over you when you feel like you're about to drown in a sea of grief, hurt, and rejection, disappointment, or despair. Here is a beautiful promise from God's Word: "The LORD your God is with you, he is mighty to save. He will take great delight in you, he will quiet you with his love, he will rejoice over you with singing" (Zephaniah 3:17). To get to the end of the day and be governed by a peace that passes all understanding is not of this world. It is like an indescribable breath of fresh sea air. The thought of God rejoicing over us with singing is *so very lovely.*

Through worship we enter into the peace that God talks about. Peace sounds so gentle, but it is a source of grand power in our lives. When we are at peace, we live life from a position of strength—running without growing weary or faint.

Understanding Will Increase

God knew we would need help understanding His vast love for us, so He promised to send the Holy Spirit to counsel us and teach us everything the Lord wants us to know (see John 14:26). The Holy Spirit will speak into our hearts only what He hears the Father say to Him. John 16:14 teaches that He will bring glory to Jesus by taking what belongs to Him and making it known to us. Beautiful, beautiful, beautiful!

Even if you don't understand much at first, it is important to keep reading the Word and keep asking God to reveal truth to you through the Holy Spirit. The Word will lead you directly to the Father's heart.

What you sow into your heart you will reap. In the midst of life, some of my most divine experiences have been when the Holy Spirit has reminded me of a promise in His Word. God's timing is always perfect. Romans 10:17 says, "Faith comes from hearing the message, and the message is heard through the word of Christ." That's why it is important to meditate on Scripture until we understand how it applies to our current circumstances. It is difficult to ignore God's leading with His promises inscribed on our hearts.

The God Gap

Nearly every Bible story of God's encounter with His people reveals a moment when God told them what He wanted them to do, and depending on their faith, they either obeyed or disobeyed. They had nothing more than a promise to help them decide which way to go.

The story of Noah's faith in God's word is one of the most amazing stories to me. God told him to build an ark big enough to hold the future of all creation because He was sending rain to destroy the earth. There is no natural way that Noah had the capacity to understand the concept of a flood. Imagine that! Imagine the ridicule Noah would have suffered over so many years as people jeered at him for building protection against a *flood*— something no one had ever seen. Noah didn't have evidence or scientific proof that rain was coming; he only had a word from God.

Abraham left the security of his homeland because God said to go to a place he would later inherit. Abraham went without even knowing where he was going! His faith increased throughout his lifetime as he acted on God's word and was rewarded with the promise God had given him.

Moses, Gideon, Barak, Samson, Jephthah, David, and Samuel—none of these men were perfect, but they all had *faith* in their God. Their proof that God had spoken to them always came *after* they acted on what they believed. There have been so many times in my life when the natural circumstances looked crazy, but God was asking me to *obey* and trust Him. This kind of situation, I feel obliged to say, is *never* comfortable.

At the beginning of one of our church's women's

conferences, I gave my eldest daughter, Amy, half a day off school so that she could come and sing in one of the sessions. Chloe, who is ten, loves soccer, Legos, and robots, and was mortified that she wasn't having half a day off so she could build robots at home! (That's my Chloe!) I said, "Honey, if you would like to come to the women's conference, you can have half the day off too!" She responded, "I am not going to a 'colour your nails' conference." (Anything 'pink' is taboo for Chloe's world; she is just not interested.)

I said, "Well, you cannot have the day off school then!" Well, I'd love to say that my angel responded with an "Okay, Mummy." But, reality is, she whined and complained while I stood my ground.

Later I came out into the hall, and Chloe was marching past me, up and down the hallway. She'd made a sign and put it on a stick. It read: "It's not fair! It's not fair! It's not fair!" She did! Mark and I went to get ready to leave, and when we came out again, "It's not fair!" posters were planted all along the hallway.

Don't you feel like doing that sometimes, though? Marching with your picketing sign "It's not fair!" for all to see? It won't feel fair sometimes. That's why you have got to love your God Gap.

There is *no* magic in making your dream become a reality. Surprise! That is just the truth of it. On one side is reality, where we are all living, working out our lives. We are walking it out, day by day, trying to do the very best we can with what is in our hands. Just faithfully walking it out. And on the *other* side is the dream! So those are the two sides, and in the middle—is *the God Gap.* I often feel that the distance from reality to the dream seems like an awfully long way. And yet there, in the God Gap, where we were designed to live, is faith . . . the substance of things hoped for, the evidence of things not seen.

One man that I have dreamed of meeting one day (maybe it will be in heaven) is Billy Graham. Just an ordinary guy, with an incredible heart after God . . . and a passion to reach the lost. And do you know how Billy Graham has been given the privilege of leading millions to Christ? By doing "life"—reality, the day-to-day existence—really well. Walking it out, one crusade at a time, one person at a time, being the hands and feet of Jesus one day at a time— sometimes in grand stadiums, sometimes to neighbors over the fence; by loving his wife, by being a father to his children. Through being faithful and passionate in his "reality," living in the God Gap, and trusting God, he has had the privilege of being able to see his dreams realized. This servant of Christ, like Nehemiah, willing to give his life away for others, has walked in divine favor, for the cause of the King.

We were in the United States on tour during the September 11, 2001, terrorist attacks. I remember that week looking at Billy Graham, who had been asked to come and address a gathering of national leaders. He got up to speak, and on the bottom of the TV screen it read: "Billy Graham—pastor to the nation." I thought about how incredible it is that while this man just faithfully did whatever God was asking him to do throughout the years of his life, God gave him the privilege of being called shepherd to the nation of America in one of its most desperate times. How inspiring.

God has gifted us to be great thinkers. The capacity of our intellect is quite remarkable. We can think on many different levels about many things at different times. But we need to learn not to manipulate circumstances to see our dreams come to pass. God-relationships are awesome, but any of us can get caught in the trap of manipulation, and that is not living in the "trusting God" area. To get into the trap of promoting yourself rather than allowing God to do it for you, is a hole you do not want to find yourself in. Opportunities that are borne out of good relationships are great, but not when they come out of using or abusing a contact to suit your own needs. Trust in the Lord with *all* your heart, and lean not on your own understanding.

Dreams Versus Goals

There is a great difference between a dream and a goal. Goals are awesome. Goals are honorable; goals are godly;

goals are noble. But with forward planning and discipline, goals are set to equip you to achieve them.

Let me challenge you with this thought: If you can figure out how you can do it, then it is not a dream. It's a goal. I tell you, I don't want to get to heaven and have God say, "Well done, my good and faithful *planner*." Just pulling off your plans is great, but I want to live in the faith realm, in the God Gap, the land of the miraculous!

Mark and I had been married for just one year when we came to Hillsong Church. There were a couple of hundred of us; none of us had much money, but we had a big dream, and we knew we served a big God. To afford our apartment, I had to help mow the lawns on our rental property so they would take some money off our rent! That was our reality—but we were happy serving God. We were really passionate about what God could do through our lives, and we were just walking it out. We are still walking it out, living in that God Gap, and are now starting to see some of the dream that was birthed all those years ago become a reality. We are starting to get a glimpse of dreams coming true.

When my two-year-old was just a baby, I was holding her in my arms one day while my older two were at school. As I watched her sleep, I said to Mark, "Honey, I feel like I am living my dream." He just looked at me, waited a moment, and said, "Well, dream bigger!" After I got over the shock, I thanked God for a man who thinks like that and who challenges my moments where I could easily be tempted to pull back and stop "pressing forward." He challenges complacency in me.

Things You Don't Want to Know About the Dream

It is *hard work*. Seeing our dreams come to pass is hard work. It takes focus. There are long hours, frustration, times of testing and stretching. When we are in the God Gap, it's scary; it doesn't feel comfortable, and it's not nice. It is not supposed to be comfortable! We need to learn to keep saying, "I can do all things through Christ who strengthens me" (Philippians 4:13 NKJV).

Sometimes when we are in our God Gap it will seem *unfair*. Sometimes our God Gap will seem not like a dream but rather our own little nightmare. There are comparisons and disappointments. We might feel we have been overlooked. There might be tragedy, which did not fit in to how we thought life would unfold. At a women's conference in 2001, one of my girl friends had just lost her five-month-old baby. And she came to the conference and cried her way through it. Do you know where she was living? In her God Gap. "Faith is the substance of things hoped for, the evidence of things not seen" (Hebrews 11:1 NKJV). Do you know where my friend was safest? In the God Gap. The

Holy Spirit is working and moving to see her dream still realized. Her dream is not over, even though it felt like her life was over. But she has had to walk through that tragedy. It will sometimes seem unfair, but God's timing is perfect. Psalm 31:14–15 says, "I trust in you, O LORD. . . . My times are in your hands." It is lovely to pray all these Scriptures when our world is going great, but we need to sow them into our hearts for when our days are not going great so that we can confess them and state the Word of God over our circumstances.

Second Corinthians 1:20–22 says, "For no matter how many promises God has made, they are 'Yes' in Christ. And so through him the 'Amen' is spoken by us to the glory of God." Not in our own strength, but *through Him* is the "Amen" spoken to the glory of God. "Now it is God who makes both us and you stand firm in Christ. He anointed us, set His seal of ownership on us, and put His Spirit in our hearts as a deposit, guaranteeing what is to come." And at the end of verse 24 it says, "Because it is by faith you stand firm." By faith! Not always easy, but by faith.

Another thing to realize is that *it's not all about you.* I know, it's a shock! God wants us healed, whole, well, strong, so we can go and minister to the brokenhearted, the hurting, and the needy. Not so we can sing worship songs forever! My natural person would love to sing and worship for days, and it would really help, heal, and make me tender before the Father, but we need to know how to bring all we learn into the process of living life well! *It's not all about me.* We need to be consumed with the needs of others. Sometimes we can be so consumed with seeing our dreams come to pass, and we can become so focused on that, that our eyes don't even see the very thing God has put in our hand, and we miss it, we miss the whole experience of the journey—being so consumed with the impossible, all that we don't have, that we forget that God has given us favor for each day, making the impossible possible.

One way to see your dreams come true is simply by making other people's dreams a reality. I love that. I love that in our worship and creative arts team I have been given the privilege of being able to help other people's dreams come true. It is hard work, and it comes at a cost. To get creative people; not just people, but creative people—a different thing altogether—working together in harmony like a well-oiled machine, under the oil of the Holy Spirit, comes at a cost. That's why heaven loves it. Unity is costly. It's all about Him, and when we understand it's all about Him and about taking others *to* Him, well, there're just no words to describe that sense of fulfillment.

Our dreams start in the unseen and will be tested there. The big things are pulled off by faithfully doing well in all the little things. And when we think we are walking well in the big things, we need to think about what the big things are made up of—lots of little things! People think we have graduated to this successful life, and I say, "Are you serious? It's just a lot more of what we have always done."

Another thing. Our dreams will live or die with our confession. If we keep saying, "I can't; I won't; I never will; my family just never told me that I could"; well, guess what? you probably won't. In the end we just have to get past all of that and say, "With God, I can." We have got to start saying, "I can; I will; I would love to; what an honor; what a privilege." Submit. And do you know what? When it comes to submission, the Bible doesn't actually ask for our opinion. Ouch! It just says to serve another's vision. I have seen so many of my dreams realized purely by serving another's vision, and as my dreams are realized more and more, my challenge will be to continue to serve another's vision. Before God and all of heaven, that is exactly what Mark and I plan to do, because that is where we will see all our dreams come true . . . in the God Gap.

When God's Word is in our hearts, our desires change.

When God's Word is in our hearts, our desires change. And I have desired some crazy things in my life! Praise God for His timing, wisdom, and *protection* over my inexperienced heart—protecting myself from my self.

> *I appeal to you therefore, brethren, and beg of you in view of [all] the mercies of God, to make a decisive dedication of your bodies—presenting all your members and faculties—as a living sacrifice, holy (devoted, consecrated) and well pleasing to God, which is your reasonable (rational, intelligent) service and spiritual worship. Do not be conformed to this world—this age, fashioned after and adapted to its external, superficial customs. But be transformed (changed) by the [entire] renewal of your mind—by its new ideals and its new attitude—so that you may prove [for yourselves] what is the good and acceptable and perfect will of God, even the thing which is good and acceptable and perfect [in His sight for you].*
>
> *For by the grace (unmerited favor of God) given to me I warn everyone among you not to estimate and think of himself more highly than he ought—not to have an exaggerated opinion of his own importance; but to rate his ability with sober judgment, each according to the degree of faith apportioned by God to him. For as in one physical body we have many parts (organs, members) and all of these parts do not have the same function or use, so we, numerous as we are, are one body in Christ, the Messiah, and individually we are parts one of another—mutually dependent on one another. Having gifts (faculties, talents, qualities) that differ according to the grace given us, let us use them: [He whose gift is] prophecy, [let him prophesy] according to the propor-*

tion of his faith; [he whose gift is] practical service, let him give himself to serving; he who teaches, to his teaching; (he who exhorts, encourages), to his exhortation; he who contributes, let him do it in simplicity and liberality; he who gives aid and superintends, with zeal and singleness of mind; he who does acts of mercy, with genuine cheerfulness and joyful eagerness. (Romans 12:1–8 AMP)

You can learn through God's Word to love living in the God Gap . . . embrace it, don't fight it . . . learn to love it.

> *Your breath of Life has overwhelmed me*
> *and set my spirit free.*
> *Your love is immeasurable,*
> *too deep to comprehend.*
> *I'm living in the embrace of heaven.*
> *And I'll never be the same again.*
> (excerpt from "Kiss of Heaven")

"I LONG *to* BE *an*
EXTRAVAGANT WORSHIPER
that GOD WOULD DISCOVER
the SONG *in* MY HEART
to BE ELABORATE,
OVER-GENEROUS, *and* WASTEFUL
in MY PURSUIT *of* HIM."

darlene zschech

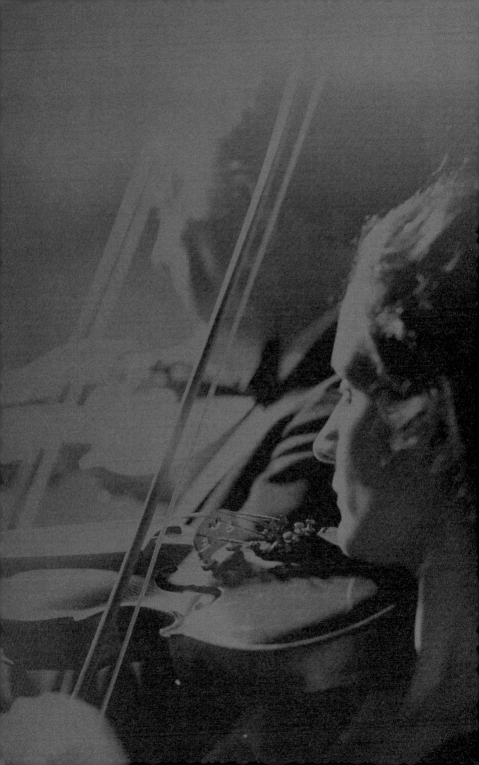

devoted to his worship

Eight

DEVOTED TO HIS WORSHIP

You alone are the LORD. *You made the heavens, even the highest heavens, and all their starry host, the earth and all that is on it, the seas and all that is in them. You give life to everything, and the multitudes of heaven worship you.*
(Nehemiah 9:6)

Inside every human being is a desire to worship! We were created to show love and to be loved, and whether you have just begun to know this beautiful Savior or you have walked with the Lord for a long time, the result of this glorious meeting of humanity with the divine is to worship. Your response to the reality of salvation is worship. Your response to the promises of His Word is worship. Your response to His greatness is to worship.

Once you know, recognize, and understand what the

Word of God promises, your natural desire will be to worship God, praising Him for who He is and all He does. Now, I understand that *every* time I speak or write, my commitment to worship is obvious. But the whole of the Bible is a call to worship—the drawing of humankind to the devotion of our Creator. It is a great key to living in wholeness and under favor.

The heart of worship implores us to bring an offering of the heart.

I was in for a lovely surprise when I came to the understanding that one of the many differences between worship and music was that worship is *inclusive, not exclusive.* The music of worship embraces every man, woman, and child. The heart of worship implores us to bring an offering of the heart, lifting our voices, and it releases whatever we have to give. It allows everyone to come as they are and participate. It is so fragrant, so pure, so beautiful! On the other hand, music was created to carry, capture, and communicate the presence of God, but over generations it has been taken out of the hands of all people and given *exclusively* into the hands of the extremely gifted, skilled, pretty, young, and brilliant—not to mention the extremely lucky. Only a few are now allowed to sing and personally enjoy contributing to the expression of music found on the planet.

God created us to enjoy fellowship with Him. Formed and lovingly fashioned in His own image, He calls us His children. We are His beloved family and heirs to all the goodness of His provision. That truth alone should fill us with desire to worship Him for His great and remarkable love that He demonstrates toward His own.

When God sent Moses to deliver the children of Israel from the oppression of slavery, He told Moses to say to Pharaoh, "This is what the LORD says: Israel is my firstborn son, and I told you, 'Let my son go, *so he may worship me*'" (Exodus 4:22–23). He didn't say, "so my people can go to work for me." He wanted His children to be free so they could spend time in His presence and worship Him. The entire endeavor of God is about connecting—His connecting with us, and our connecting with Him.

As we express to Him our adoration, obedience, praise, and thanksgiving in worship, the reality of His presence is quite breathtaking—overwhelmingly glorious. I know it is hard to understand or comprehend God's great love toward us. Yet when we worship Him for what little we do understand, His love is so geared toward us that I'm often aware of the angel armies gathered in a chorus of devotion as our Lord's face shines upon us.

In worship I often find that my concerns for that day simply melt away in the light of His glory and grace. Allow yourself to be honest before Him in worship, and He will *always* be faithful to respond.

In worship I often find that my concerns for that day simply melt away in the light of His glory and grace.

The presence of God is a great leveler. Imagine—we limp along on our darkest day, full of arguments and reasons why we can't do something, but through a choice, a moment, we become aware again of His magnificent presence in worship. Divine love, limited only by our perception, not His.

The ninth chapter of Nehemiah records the many works of God that the children of Israel remembered when they worshiped the Lord. I encourage you to read the entire chapter, but verse 6 begins, "You alone are the LORD. You made the heavens, even the highest heavens, and all their starry host, the earth and all that is on it, the seas and all that is in them. You give life to everything, and the multitudes of heaven worship you."

In their time of worship the Israelites gave thanks for all they understood about God and for all the promises He had fulfilled through His covenant to Abraham. They remembered that He sent miraculous signs and wonders against Pharaoh and divided the sea before them so they could escape Pharaoh's army. They remembered that He led them with a pillar of cloud by day and a pillar of fire by night. He gave them laws that were righteous and fed them bread from heaven and water from the rock. Even when they were unfaithful, God was gracious, compassionate, slow to anger, and abounding in love. They remembered that He never deserted them, even when they made an idol to worship instead of Him and committed awful blasphemies. They remembered how patient God was with them and how He had sent prophets to warn and lead them. But in His great mercy He never put an end to them or abandoned them, because He is a gracious and merciful God.

Jesus said, "Yet a time is coming and has now come when the true worshipers will worship the Father in spirit and truth, for they are the kind of worshipers the Father seeks. God is spirit, and his worshipers must worship in spirit and in truth" (John 4:23–24). It's not difficult to understand why the Lord wants us to worship Him in spirit and truth, for our spirits will only be complete when found in intimate relationship with Christ and the reigning truth of Jesus. Once we know the truth, we are literally set free. Set free to praise; set free to love and be loved; set free to live! Worshiping God in truth keeps us aware of His amazing love for us.

David majestically describes why the Lord is worthy of our worship:

Shout for joy to the LORD, *all the earth.*
Worship the LORD *with gladness; come before him with joyful songs.*
Know that the LORD *is God. It is he who made us, and we are his; we are his people, the sheep of his pasture.*
Enter his gates with thanksgiving and his courts with praise; give thanks to him and praise his name.
For the LORD *is good and his love endures forever; his faithfulness continues through all generations.* (Psalm 100:1–5)

Worship Brings Change and Sets People Free

It was through moments of worship, lovingly singing and praising my Father and my Savior, that God renewed my heart, my inner man came alive to His voice, and the reality of my life not being my own became a joy—even a relief. I had been so busy working for God, needing to do something for Him—a typical response from someone with poor self-esteem. But He has continually reassured me in that atmosphere of praise that what He wants from me first is my thankful heart. With time and through building a relationship with God, my mind has been slowly renewed to understand that His costly love is freely given. The more

I understand this, the freer I become to serve, obey, and worship my Lord.

If we could see into the supernatural realm as we praise God, I believe we would be surprised at how much is being challenged and changed in the natural world through our acts of worship. The Word promises that God inhabits the praises of His people, and where God dwells there is no darkness (see 1 John 1:5). This means that if genuine praise is being declared, then any presence of evil must flee.

After my spiritual eyes were opened through salvation, I was amazed the first time I saw believers praising God corporately. I had seen Christians singing together before, but once I was saved, I never really heard music the same way ever again. I didn't understand it until much later in life, but in my initial years of praising God with other believers, I started to understand and value the dynamics of corporate worship. There is tremendous power in coming together and shouting His praises in unity—it is indescribable.

Worshiping God confronts deposits of selfishness and impurities in our hearts. The more we encounter God, the less room there is for concerns over our own needs and imperfections. The less concerned we are about ourselves, the more aware we become of the Lord's awesome presence. I'm *always* aware of divine favor in worship. Every time I decide to lift my hands and declare His majesty, He meets me, and I find Him again.

Worship Softens the Heart

I watched a documentary once that talked about today's children who are hurting. It was primarily about children of divorce and the great inner resilience these children have developed through surviving brokenness at such a tender age. This particular program had branded them as "flat-liners" because there is so much going on in their beautiful hearts, but so much more than they should have to carry, that their little hearts have become hard and unresponsive. It even asked the question about this generation's need for extreme sport, extreme experiences—whether life needed to be lived on the edge to promote the heart to feel again! Interesting.

Love is always a risk. Our human hearts can only handle so much hurt before a survival mechanism kicks in and we put walls around our feelings and develop a hardness of heart. Unfortunately, this hardness doesn't just prevent hurt from entering; it also creates great complications when it comes to giving or receiving any emotion sacrificially—including love.

As I watched this documentary, the Spirit of God spoke to me about the continued need to reach young people and establish the song of the Lord firmly in their lives. I know how easy it is to develop a hard heart at a young age, and I also know how patient our beautiful Lord is as we journey with Him in unraveling and softening our hearts again so we can be open to receive His love.

In worship, the heavily constructed walls of protection I had built around my heart were removed. My heart of stone became a heart of flesh. Such a miracle!

We don't worship to feel good; worship declares God's reigning power into our lives.

Worship teaches our hearts, young and old alike, that there is an answer to alleviate pain. There is another way to live, by running to the Father and bowing before Him with adoration and praise! "Worth-ship."

Worship Changes the Atmosphere

Praise and worship is active, not passive. It is a decision of the heart, the mind, and the will to enter His gates into God's presence. We don't worship to feel good; worship declares God's reigning power into our lives.

This is confirmed in 2 Chronicles 5:12–14, when all the Levites who were musicians stood beside the altar and played cymbals, harps, and lyres while 120 priests sounding trumpets accompanied them. The trumpeters and singers sang "in unison, as with one voice," their "praise and thanks to the LORD. Then the temple of the LORD was filled with a cloud, and the priests could not perform their service because of the cloud, for the glory of the LORD filled the temple of God." That is a beautiful picture of praise welcoming the presence of God.

Every person, regardless of his or her personality type, from reserved to flamboyant, can enjoy the act of praise.

We start our corporate worship services with praise because the Word tells us to enter God's courts with thanksgiving and praise (see Psalm 100:4). The word *praise* in Hebrew is *tehillah* and is a laudation; specifically (concretely) a hymn. It is derived from the Hebrew word *halal*, which means to shine; hence, to make a show, to boast; and thus to be (clamorously) foolish; to rave; causatively, to celebrate; also to stultify. (What a cool word!)

A call to praise is an opportunity to boast of the Lord, celebrate Him, commend Him, and give Him glory. Every person, regardless of his or her personality type, from reserved to flamboyant, can enjoy the act of praise.

Praise fills the house with joy. Praise brings heaven's dominion on earth. James 5:13 says, "Is anyone happy? Let him sing songs of praise." People without God need to hear the praise of God's people. Praise at home; praise in your car; make it a lifelong habit.

Isaiah 14:12–15 tells of the fall of Lucifer. It describes him as the morning star and says that he wanted to be higher than the Most High. The atmosphere of heaven is worship, and Lucifer was the overseer of worship. Pride started to do its ugly work, and Lucifer and his friends were cast eternally from the presence of the Almighty.

But think about it. Lucifer, who was in charge of the atmosphere, has again tried to dominate the atmosphere of the earth, bringing despair and heartache, reigning in fear straight from the pit of hell. It is no wonder that in Isaiah it says "that in these days praise and righteousness will spring up" (62:11–12). It must; it must! The prevailing atmosphere of earth as it is in heaven must be the kingdom of God. *You must take your place, take your place and stand up and declare that our God is great and greatly to be praised!* That is why we must understand that we have been given this mission and mandate to be leaders in life on the earth today—not worship leaders, but all of us as lead worshipers!

The presence of God is here. Do you know that? We say things like, "We are going to get together in worship, and we are going to shout, and then God will come." Well, God came, and He is still here. God loves us; God is here whether you like it or not. The presence of God is here. We are now born of the Spirit. So wherever we go, God comes with us; you can't escape it. Psalm 139:7 says, "Where can I go from your Spirit? Where can I flee from your presence?" This is David overwhelmed by God's grand capacity *to be.* "If I go up to the heavens, you are there; if I make my bed in the depths, you are there. If I rise on the wings of the dawn, if I settle on the far side of the sea, even there your hand will guide me, your right hand will hold me fast" (Psalm 139:8–10). God is here, even when you are totally unaware; God is at work all over the earth today.

Our world needs Jesus,

and our world needs joy.

Let praise change the atmosphere of your life, your home, and your church. Praise establishes joy among God's people. Joy can be the emotional currency of every Christian. Nehemiah 8:10 says, "The joy of the LORD is your strength."

Our world needs Jesus, and our world needs joy. Our homes and our churches should be full of joy unspeakable and full of glory. Rather than the world's dim light of glory, we should demonstrate the joy that only Jesus can bring—infectious, genuine, atmosphere-changing joy.

As we quoted earlier, "Shout with joy to God, all the earth! Sing the glory of his name; make his praise glorious! Say to God, 'How awesome are your deeds! So great is your power that your enemies cringe before you. All the earth bows down to you; they sing praise to you, they sing praise to your name.' *Selah*" (Psalm 66:1–4). Stop and think about that. The Word commands that as we shout for joy to God, all the earth bows down to Him and sings praise to Him.

Jesus was lifted up from the earth on a cross so He could draw all men unto himself. As we praise His name and boast of His goodness to others, we point unbelievers to the cross, where Jesus can meet their needs too.

We ought to be extravagant in our love to our God. I cannot help myself in expressing my passion for worship. I used to be quite mindful of what others thought of my own method of leading worship. But praise God, I am far more committed to truth than style.

In worship, our anxieties are supernaturally exchanged for God's provision of health for our nerves and bones (see Proverbs 3:7–8).

We ought to be extravagant in our worship, because the Father is always extravagant toward us. He longs for our heart of worship. I often sense that God is smiling as we come before Him in worship. There is nothing sweeter than feeling the Holy Spirit settle upon us like gentle rain as our hearts dance before the Lord.

IF *the* LORD DELIGHTS *in a* MAN'S WAY,

HE MAKES HIS STEPS FIRM.

THOUGH HE STUMBLE,

HE WILL NOT FALL,

for the LORD UPHOLDS HIM

with HIS HAND.

psalm 37:24

devoted to his walk

Nine

DEVOTED TO HIS WALK

Yesterday is gone. Tomorrow has not yet come. We
have only today. Let us begin!

—Mother Teresa

Walking with Jesus is the greatest privilege of my life—
never alone, abiding in Him, and learning to rest in the
shadow of His wings. I love to walk, to exercise, to be
reminded of the goodness of God as I take in the surroundings, as I "stride it out"! Part of our design is to walk—in
the natural and in the spiritual—to commit to the next
step, taking us where we need to go.

Singing magnificent songs about the Lord is fantastic,
but it's not enough. True worship is a daily lifestyle that
honors God. Living to demonstrate His character to others
is about taking another step toward reaching our God-
given dreams.

Jesus taught in Mark 7:6–7, "Isaiah was right when he prophesied about you hypocrites; as it is written: 'These people honor me with their lips, but their hearts are far from me. They worship me in vain; their teachings are but rules taught by men.'" Solomon, the wisest man who ever lived, said, "I know that it will be well with those who (reverently) fear God, who revere and worship Him, realizing His *continual* presence" (Ecclesiastes 8:12 AMP).

Singing magnificent songs about the Lord is fantastic, but it's not enough. True worship is a daily lifestyle that honors God.

How many times have you heard a great message or read an amazing Scripture and at the time thought to yourself, *That is for me; I'm going to make changes,* but then didn't do anything about it?

> *Anyone who listens to the word but does not do what it says is like a man who looks at his face in a mirror and, after looking at himself, goes away and immediately forgets what he looks like. But the man who looks intently into the*

perfect law that gives freedom, and continues to do this, not forgetting what he has heard, but doing it—he will be blessed in what he does. (James 1:23–25)

So the first work He calls us to is a work in our hearts. Then we're to offer ourselves as "instruments of righteousness" (Romans 6:13) to serve in that Great Commission of sharing Jesus. Jesus said of the Father, "To love him with all your heart, with all your understanding and with all your strength, and to love your neighbor as yourself is more important than all burnt offerings and sacrifices" (Mark 12:33).

The Message Bible explains superbly what God wants from us,

So here's what I want you to do, God helping you: Take your everyday, ordinary life—your sleeping, eating, going-to-work, and walking-around life—and place it before God as an offering. Embracing what God does for you is the best thing you can do for him. Don't become so well-adjusted to your culture that you fit into it without even thinking. Instead, fix your attention on God. You'll be changed from the inside out. Readily recognize what He wants from you, and quickly respond to it. Unlike the culture around you, always dragging you down to its level of immaturity, God brings the best out of you, develops well-formed maturity in you. (Romans 12:1–2)

We're to renew our minds to God's way of thinking, staying alert to His continual presence, listening for the Father's voice, and worshiping Him with our obedience. This awareness will change how we treat our spouse, our children, our friends, and our co-workers. This is what the walk looks like: step by step, faithfully walking well in our own shoes in the so-called mundane, for if the favor of God was only reserved for those special moments, well, it would only amount to a handful of days over the span of a lifetime. An awareness of God's presence makes us respond with His love in the marketplace, in the schoolyard, wherever we happen to find ourselves.

An awareness of God's presence

makes us respond with His love

in the marketplace, in the schoolyard,

wherever we happen to find ourselves.

Proverbs 6:16–19 lists the seven things that God hates. Notice how all of them relate to how we treat people around us. He hates arrogance, lies, murderers, evil plots, wicked goals, deceit, and troublemakers.

Genuinely loving people means more to God than any worshipful sacrifice we could offer to Him. All that He requires of us is "to act justly and to love mercy and to walk humbly with [our] God" (Micah 6:8). Walking out our faith is about simply being ready to react with justice, demonstrate kindness, and esteem others on His behalf.

Be eager to imitate Christ's humility. The Word says, "In a humble (gentle, modest) spirit receive and welcome the Word which implanted and rooted [in your hearts] contains the power to save your souls" (James 1:21 AMP). Most people living extraordinary lives are just ordinary people who continually (on a daily, sometimes minute-by-minute basis), humbly make God choices to walk well. You'll always know the life of a humble man, as grace on him is abundant. God's favor shines on those who "walk and live habitually in the (Holy) Spirit—responsive to and controlled and guided by the Spirit" (Galatians 5:16 AMP).

If we are walking with God, the fruit of the Holy Spirit should be evident in our relationships with others. When love, joy, peace, patience, kindness, benevolence, faithfulness, gentleness, and self-control emanate from our hearts, we have become living sacrifices to the Lord. Responding to trials with these virtues pleases the Lord.

> *If we live by the (Holy) Spirit, let us also walk by the Spirit.—If by the (Holy) Spirit we have our life [in God], let us go forward walking in line, our conduct controlled by the Spirit. Let us not become vainglorious and self-conceited, competitive and challenging and provoking and irritating to one another, envying and being jealous of one another.* (Galatians 5:25–26 AMP)

The Holy Spirit offers himself to us as our companion and guide. John 14:26 says, "But the Comforter (Counselor, Helper, Intercessor, Advocate, Strengthener, Standby), the Holy Spirit, Whom the Father will send in My name [in My place, to represent Me and act on My behalf], He will teach you all things. And He will cause you to recall—will remind you of, bring to your remembrance—everything I have told you" (AMP).

The more we know of God's Word, the more the Holy Spirit can use God's truth to direct us in our daily walk.

The more we know of God's Word, the more the Holy Spirit can use God's truth to direct us in our daily walk. God made powerful promises to His people if they walked with Him, saying,

*If you walk in My statutes and keep My commandments
so as to carry them out, then I shall give you rains in their
season, so that the land will yield its produce and the trees
of the field will bear their fruit. Indeed, your threshing will
last for you until grape gathering, and grape gathering will
last until sowing time. You will thus eat your food to the
full and live securely in your land.*

*I shall also grant peace in the land, so that you may lie
down with no one making you tremble. I shall also elimi-
nate harmful beasts from the land, and no sword will pass
through your land.* (Leviticus 26:3–6 NASB)

Obedience Is a Decision of the Heart

In biblical times, walking was one of the main meth-
ods of transportation. If you could walk well, you could
travel farther! *Selah.* Walk well, travel farther—sounds
good to me (and rather healthy at the same time!). As a
new Christian, I thought obedience meant following the
laws and rules of the church, and so I did—more out of
my need to please than my longing to bless the heart of
God.

Under the Old Testament covenant, disobedience to
the law ultimately led to being stoned to death. People who
didn't submit to authority died! Obedience was probably
easier then, when you consider, "Life, or painful death?
Gee, I'll do the obedience thing!"

But in this new life in Christ, again, obedience is an issue of the heart. It is not a fact-based decision; it's a faith-based decision. We obey the Lord because we trust Him, regardless of what we can see. We learn not to look through our natural eyes, but to look at His requests through the eyes of the Spirit.

Charles Swindoll said, "The very best proof of your love to the Lord is obedience—nothing more, nothing less, and nothing else."

Obedience that endures to the end is a matter of setting our will to follow God. Remember that favor for this walk requires endurance and persistence, *not perfection*! Hallelujah!

When Jesus called His disciples together, He told them that the world hated Him and would consequently hate them. He told them this so they would not be discouraged if they were persecuted for demonstrating His love and salvation to others. Jesus said, if someone slaps you, turn the other cheek. Forgive your enemies and do good to those who persecute you (see Matthew 5:38–47).

What? This kind of obedience is not for the faint-hearted. Obedient love requires the nurturing of a mother's love together with the determination of a warrior. We need to know how to *adore* and how to *war*, strong in love because we understand how much He loves us.

Obedient love requires the nurturing

of a mother's love together

with the determination of a warrior.

In our weakness, He shows His greatest power. God is at His best when I am at my worst.

Two Women Served Jesus

Every believer knows well the story of Martha and Mary in Luke 10:38–42 and how they both wanted to serve Jesus. Martha served Jesus through a work of the flesh; Mary served Him through a work of her heart.

When Jesus and His disciples came to their village, Martha catered to what she thought *He needed,* but she was too busy to ask Him what *He wanted* because she made a fact-based decision to serve Him. Unexpected guests needed food, she reasoned. But soon the anxious, over-worked Martha needed help. So she finally came to Jesus and said, "Lord, don't you care that my sister has left me to do the work by myself? Tell her to help me!"

The Lord replied, "Martha, Martha . . . you are worried and upset about many things, but only one thing is needed. Mary has chosen what is better, and it will not be taken away from her" (Luke 10:40–42). Martha didn't know that if she devoted her whole heart to the Lord, He could have fed all of her guests with a piece of bread and taken up enough leftovers to last her for days.

Mary, also eager to serve Him, didn't *do* anything *seen*, but the need in her heart drove her to the feet of her Lord. Yet her act of obedient devotion has ministered to every generation that has lived in the two thousand years since that definitive day.

Mary may have never understood in her own lifetime how far-reaching her decision was when she chose to seek God at the cost of laying her works aside. Martha's walk looked like work, while Mary's walk, at that moment, looked like devotion.

The reward of God's favor on a heart wholly devoted to Him is beyond our imagination.

The reward of God's favor on a heart wholly devoted to Him is beyond our imagination. Once you walk and live in the power of His tangible presence, anything other than living in Him does not even come close to bringing satisfaction.

"You don't have *to* have

a college degree *to* serve.

You don't have *to* make your

subject *and* your verb agree *to* serve.

You don't have *to* know

about Plato *and* Aristotle *to* serve.

You don't have *to* know Einstein's

theory *of* relativity *to* serve.

You only need *a* heart full *of* grace.

A soul generated by love.

And you can be that servant."

martin luther king, jr.

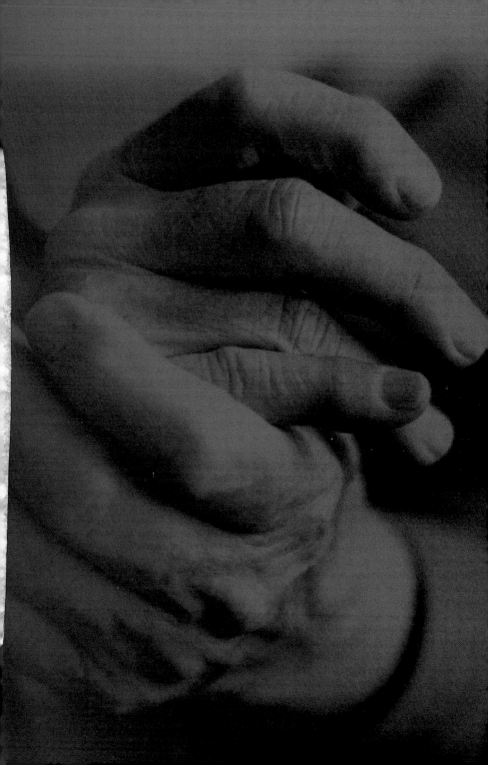

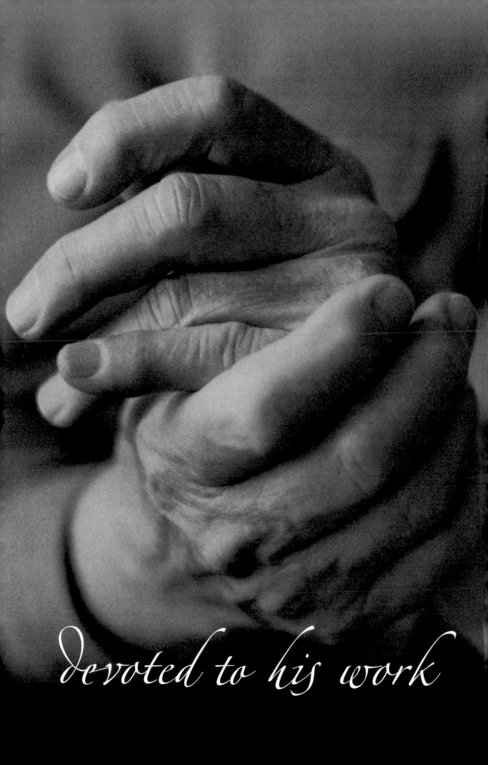

devoted to his work

Ten

DEVOTED TO HIS WORK

God has work for believers in every arena of life. We are all parts of the body of Christ, and though called to different professions and positions, we are all commissioned to "go into all the world and preach the good news to all creation" (Mark 16:15).

God has fulfilling work for scientists and mathematicians. He has assignments for poets and musicians, and for architects, sculptors, pilots, painters, and administrators. Athletes are called to the work of the Lord as well as dancers, surgeons, caretakers, mothers, fathers, teachers, and entertainers. Of this we can be certain: God has something wonderful He would like to do through each of us to bring hope to the human condition.

We are to be *doers* of the Word. Ephesians 2:1–7 teaches that we were lifeless, dead in our transgressions, and we had the habit of walking along in our sins, following the ways of the world. But because God loves us and is rich in mercy, He made us alive with Christ.

Good works do not save, but we are clearly "created in Christ Jesus to do good works, which God prepared in advance for us to do" (Ephesians 2:10). I believe that to love God with our *whole* heart is to receive faith through His Word, express relationship and friendship with Him through worship, receive His unmerited favor as we walk through life, and fulfill the work we are called to do by testifying of His intimate and amazing love.

God has something wonderful He would like to do through each of us to bring hope to the human condition.

We All Have a Place in the Body of Christ

I also believe that we are to offer our gifts and talents to the support of a local church body so we can contribute our individual gifts to serve corporate needs that are bigger than ourselves. God designed us with a need for each other.

He said that it wasn't good for man to be alone (see Genesis 2:18).

So many times I hear people say, "But why do I need to go to church? God can teach me at home. He can heal me at home. He can meet my needs no matter where I am." That is true, He can, but He also encourages us to *never* forsake the getting together of the saints, building each other up in the most holy faith. Hebrews 10:24–25 says, "And let us consider how we may spur one another on toward love and good deeds. Let us not give up meeting together, as some are in the habit of doing, but let us encourage one another—and all the more as you see the Day approaching."

If you are standing on the outside of truly enjoying community and experiencing the reality of God's presence, if you are only looking at it working in others, your emotions can easily swing between doubt and desire. It's easy to watch people worshiping God and being involved in the house of God and question the validity of their experience, wondering if they are simply "overemotional." But once you abandon yourself to give *all* of your heart and *all* of your thoughts to the Lord, you find there is no shame in praising, loving, and serving Him in the presence of others. In fact, quite the opposite is true.

In return, Jesus promised, "Whoever acknowledges me before men, I will also acknowledge him before my Father in heaven" (Matthew 10:32). Perhaps that is why bonds are so easily broken in people as they worship God in one accord with a company of other believers.

Sometimes God's presence is so strong in corporate worship services that I can hardly remain standing. Once you experience that power, you never want to return to vain works of the flesh again. You know that you were born for the purpose of worshiping God and serving Him as part of His corporate body. When we share the work of the Lord with others, we find that His yoke truly is easy, and His burden is light (see Matthew 11:29–30).

Working under the grace of His favor is definitely like being kissed by heaven.

Using your natural gifts and talents to serve the Lord by building up others in His faith is more wonderful than I'd dare try to describe. Allow the Lord to be evident in your life, and you will shine. Working under the grace of His favor is definitely like being kissed by heaven.

Gifts Are Given to Serve Others

Jesus said that if you want to be great in the kingdom of God you must serve others, and "serve wholeheartedly, as if you were serving the Lord, not men, because you know that the Lord will reward everyone for whatever good he does, whether he is slave or free" (Ephesians 6:7–8). Serving another man's vision is one of those powerful principles of God that doesn't seem quite right to the natural mind. It doesn't make sense to watch others receive acclaim while you go on unnoticed for your contribution. But it's amazing how God honors the person who serves another unselfishly. In fact, I would say that working with joy, in the shadows, is probably one of the most valuable experiences in life.

Serving another man's vision is one of those powerful principles of God that doesn't seem quite right to the natural mind.

Paul wrote to Timothy about the need to "aim at and pursue righteousness—all that is virtuous and good, right living, conformity to the will of God in thought, word, and deed. [And aim at and pursue] faith, love, [and] peace—which is harmony and concord with others—in fellowship with all [Christians], who call upon the Lord out of a pure heart" (2 Timothy 2:22 AMP).

Every act of service to the whole body is valuable, and part of God's divine plan. "So neither he who plants nor he who waters is anything, but only God, who makes things grow. The man who plants and the man who waters have one purpose, and each will be rewarded according to his own labor. For we are God's fellow workers; you are God's field, God's building" (1 Corinthians 3:7–9). The secular world needs to see the kingdom, the church, the bride as strong and unified with an uncompromising message of faith, hope, and love.

The Word says that all of "creation waits in eager expectation for the sons of God to be revealed" (Romans 8:19). When Christians understand who they are in Christ and operate in the creative gifts that God has bestowed upon them, they will see an unprecedented outpouring of God's favor on their lives that will bring a harvest of souls into the kingdom.

Unity and agreement bring God's favor and power into our prayers. "And I pray that you, being rooted and established in love, may have power, *together with all the saints,* to grasp how wide and long and high and deep is the love of Christ, and to know this love that surpasses knowledge—that you may be filled to the measure of all the fullness of God" (Ephesians 3:17–19).

I have seen again and again from firsthand experience in our own church team, filled with people who are committed to *His work,* that there is such favor granted to those willing to pay the price of unity—hard work and sacrifice. It is costly. It can reveal all the things you don't love about yourself. It takes such an unnatural measure of selflessness. But the fruit of it is truly a remarkable testimony to the grace and favor of the King.

FOR SURELY, O LORD,
    YOU BLESS *the* RIGHTEOUS;
YOU SURROUND THEM *with*
    YOUR FAVOR *as with a* SHIELD.

psalm 5:12

keep your way pure

Eleven

KEEP YOUR WAY PURE

A ctress Lily Tomlin was quoted in a magazine saying, "I always wanted to be somebody, but I
should have been more specific." I love that. Her
humor reminds us to establish clear objectives early in
life—before we spend too much time on the wrong pursuits.

Before I gave my heart to God, I was driven to find
success merely through the work of my hands. Once I
learned to trust in God's favor, I could rest, knowing the
work He does in me will lead me in the right direction. I
still work hard, laboring for excellence. In some ways, trusting in Him inspires me to do more, and knowing God has
a plan for my life keeps me going in a straight path toward
the prize of His high calling (see Philippians 3:14). Jesus

said, "Where your treasure is, there your heart will be also" (Luke 12:34).

King David asked the question, "How can a young man keep his way pure?" The answer: "By living according to your word. I seek you with all my heart; do not let me stray from your commands. I have hidden your word in my heart that I might not sin against you" (Psalm 119:9–11). I treasure the favor that God has given to our worship team. I treasure His Word, and I pray that I will not sin against Him.

One of the most difficult temptations when following the Lord, and the most dangerous to the flow of favor, is our own pride. When God's favor is shining on us, it tends to put us in the spotlight of attention. The temptation to enjoy honor too much can steal away the beauty of God's unmerited favor. As soon as we begin to think of ourselves as "God's gift to the world," we begin to slip from the glory He wants to bestow upon us. We must never forget who gave the gifts and what they are for, or we may be tempted to take full credit for it ourselves or sell it cheaply.

David's prayer in Psalm 51:10–13 is a powerful request to lay before God.

Create in me a pure heart, O God, and renew a steadfast spirit within me.

Do not cast me from your presence or take your Holy Spirit from me.

Restore to me the joy of your salvation and grant me a willing spirit, to sustain me.

Then I will teach transgressors your ways, and sinners will turn back to you.

Success is a great indicator of what is really in a person's heart.

Success is a great indicator of what is really in a person's heart. True motives are often revealed when honor is bestowed on someone. I have heard so many times about hardship revealing the truth about you, but I can tell you that success will too!

Speak, that I may see thee. . . . The metal of a bell is known by its sound. Birds reveal their nature by their song. Owls cannot sing the carol of a lark, nor can the nightingale hoot like an owl. Let us then, weigh and watch our words, lest our speech should prove us to be foreigners. (Socrates)

Solomon wrote of life's purpose in Ecclesiastes 12:13, saying, "All has been heard. The end of the matter is, Fear God—know that He is, *revere and worship Him,*—and keep

His commandments, for *this is the whole of man [the full original purpose of his creation,* the object of God's providence, the root of character, the foundation of all happiness, the adjustment to all inharmonious circumstances and conditions under the sun], and the whole duty for every man" (AMP). What an *awesome* Scripture!

My heart is not for sale. God has claimed *all* of it to be His own. My life purpose is to revere and worship the Lord, as is the purpose of every person on earth (even though everyone doesn't know that).

God speaks those five words, "You are not for sale," to all of us. Our hearts have been bought with a great price, and they are not up for grabs. No deals, no financial contracts, no momentary pleasure, no earthly offer can compare to the fellowship that is given to those who love God with their whole heart.

The Message Bible says, "Don't love the world's ways. Don't love the world's goods. Love of the world squeezes out love for the Father. Practically everything that goes on in the world—wanting your own way, wanting everything for yourself, wanting to appear important—has nothing to do with the Father. It only isolates you from Him. The world and all its wanting, wanting, wanting is on the way out—but whoever does what God wants is set for eternity" (1 John 2:15–17).

How Much Is Your Birthright Worth?

I was reminded of the story of Esau, who, because he was hungry and because he'd just had a big day, sold his birthright to his brother Jacob—for a bowl of stew! Esau had a temporary problem that he chose to solve with a permanent regret (see Genesis 25:29–34).

Sometimes when the squeeze is on, when the pressure is almost too much to bear, it is easy to look for quick solutions, a way out, an "exit clause." But as my pastor says, if an opportunity looks too good to be true, it probably is! Don't sell your birthright for the equivalent of a bowl of beans.

Esau had a temporary problem that he chose to solve with a permanent regret.

Favor is found in tenacity; favor is revealed in remaining steadfast. "But he who keeps [treasures] His Word—who bears in mind His precepts, who observes His message in its entirety—truly in him has the love of and for God been perfected (completed, reached maturity). By this we may perceive and know and recognize and be sure that we are in Him: Whoever says he abides in Him ought—as a personal debt—to walk and conduct himself in the same way in which He walked and conducted Himself" (1 John 2:5–6 AMP).

In Paul's first letter to Timothy, he imparts the Word of God to the church, calling us to pray every way we know how for everyone we know. We're to pray for rulers and governments to rule well so we can live peaceful and quiet lives (see 1 Timothy 2:1–2). *The Message* Bible says,

> *This is the way our Savior God wants us to live.*
>
> *He wants not only us but* everyone *saved, you know, everyone to get to know the truth* we've *learned: that there's one God and only one, and one Priest-Mediator between God and us—Jesus, who offered himself in exchange for everyone held captive by sin, to set them all free. Eventually the news is going to get out. This and this only has been my appointed work: getting this news to those who have never heard of God, and explaining how it works by simple faith and plain truth.* (1 Timothy 2:3–4)

Serve God Alone

"No one can serve two masters. Either he will hate the one and love the other, or he will be devoted to the one and despise the other. You cannot serve both God and Money" (Matthew 6:24). It is sad to watch tremendously gifted people selling themselves short, looking for a deal—

their piece of the action! They never receive all they could from their present opportunity because they are always on the lookout for the next best thing. They are faithful if it benefits them, looking for a path to somewhere else, not knowing that what they are truly seeking can only be found in the Creator, not the created.

As soon as we begin to believe that our talent is self-generated and not a gift from God, we lose sight of the work of grace that God has bestowed upon us. I think all of us can battle with *pride* in different dimensions. That little five-letter word, though no one wants to talk about it, will undo you if you allow it to take hold in your life. But when it becomes the primary condition of your heart, that is when it will plunder you, and the life you dream of living can never become all you desire it to be.

How can you tell if pride has crept into your life? First, you are *easily offended.* You judge things by natural surroundings and understanding. Taking offense is easy, but it is always a choice! Often it is because you do not understand the sovereign timing and hand of God on your world, because if you know and trust in God and know He holds your life in the core of not only His hand but His heart, then no matter what goes on, you will stay strong and not take offense. You will shake it off and learn to walk on.

Over the last one hundred years a lot of people in

ministry have fallen or simply walked away because of pride that was rooted in offense. Sometimes just one offense actually stole their future. We read in the Psalms, "Who may ascend the hill of the LORD? Who may stand in his holy place?" (Psalm 24:3). What is it? "He who has clean hands and a pure heart" (v. 4). If the clean hands have been dirty, Jesus sees them as clean through the power of the Cross. And a pure heart. Do not let your heart be burdened and heavy, because it will end up being a stronghold that will tie you and secure you to your past.

Another way of telling if pride has crept into your life is through *self-centeredness*—it never allows you to see the big picture. There are so many times when the Word actually says, "Lift up your head" or "Lift up your eyes." It requires action—your obedience and the submitting of your will. Lifting up your eyes takes your focus off yourself and puts it on the faithfulness of God—His plan, His purpose, His timing.

If pride has crept in, you will start *fighting for your rights*—fighting for your place, your position, and your prominence. The disciples were spirited and quite opinionated, and some of them were quite prideful. Whenever they started to fight for their rights, what did Jesus do? He walked away. He would not allow it near Him.

Psalm 90:8 says our secret sins have to be brought into light in the presence of God. You can tell pride has crept in if there is a lot of *secrecy* attached to your life. People think secrecy creates mystery and a bit of awe. Mystique is not created like that. Mystique is created by wonder; mystique is created by your being tapped into the source of the Creator of heaven and earth. There is something about wonder and staying in the light of His presence that brings mystique to your world. Secrecy only creates confusion.

If pride has crept in, you start to become *isolated*— you pull back. It can happen for a lot of reasons. You might be feeling inadequate; often it is because you feel misunderstood or disappointed. Disappointment is difficult for anyone. But you have to give it over to God or it will become a little root of bitterness, and bit by bit you will pull back, become less available, and disconnect from friendships, until suddenly someone is reaching out, and your hand is now in your pocket, refusing to reach out. Isolation. A wise man stays in the company of the wise (Proverbs 13:20).

Another sign of pride is *needing to be served* rather than serving others. There is a clarion call—an urgent appeal— that has gone out across the earth in the last few years, and people of all races, ages, talents, and gifting are starting to come and take their place in the kingdom. But where it goes wrong is when it changes to a need to be served rather than to serve. What will set you apart is your willingness to come alongside, your willingness to share, your willingness to serve others, your willingness to give away your life so others may find it.

You can keep pride from controlling your life. To live without pride means learning the power of saying, "I trust you, Lord, even though I don't understand."

1. *Be clothed with humility.* Humility is freedom from pride or arrogance. It's a modest estimate of one's own worth. It's a sense of one's own unworthiness due to imperfection and sinfulness. It is *not* thinking of yourself as being lower than a worm, because if we are going to lead people, we have to be out in front. But leading is all about taking people by the hand and pointing them to Jesus—not showing off our own wonderfulness!

Often God's plan causes us to face hurts and attitudes we don't want to face.

Often God's plan causes us to face hurts and attitudes we don't want to face. Refusing to deal with issues will not free us from the root issues in our lives. It's a bit like the ostrich theory: Stick your head in the sand and just hope and pray the problem will go away! This will only give us temporary relief, while the core of the problem remains untouched. It is the path of humility and honesty that leads to healing and spiritual maturity. Pride cannot travel this path. It can only be traveled by those who desire peace, whatever it may take. It is the road that leads to life: "Blessed are the peacemakers, for they will be called sons of God" (Matthew 5:9).

2. *Let go.* You either believe God or you don't. And that is the journey of salvation that we all travel and where we will grow. We grow in our understanding of His faithfulness. I have seen God faithful in my life so many times, I would be a fool to think that He couldn't do what He has promised. My purpose is to say yes to the voice of God.

To enjoy God's blessing, all we need to do is accept His invitation, saying, *Yes, I will follow you anywhere you choose to lead me. I will come to your supper. I will let your glory shine through my life. I love you, Lord, more than life.* No spectacular talent is required for admission to His celebration.

It's not that God can't use incredibly gifted people, but Jesus said, " 'Indeed, it is easier for a camel to go through the eye of a needle than for a rich man to enter the kingdom of God.' Those who heard this asked, 'Who then can be saved?' Jesus replied, 'What is impossible with men is possible with God' " (Luke 18:25–27).

James 4:4–6 explains, "Don't you know that friendship with the world is hatred toward God? Anyone who chooses to be a friend of the world becomes an enemy of God. Or do you think Scripture says without reason that the spirit he caused to live in us envies intensely? But he gives us more grace." Pride has a similar way of thwarting potential, similar to trying to light a fire using wet wood.

For years I struggled with this sense of the "call of God" on my life. I had no revelation of living in the righteousness of Christ. As a wife, a mum, how was I to do well all that I felt I could do? I was also quite stubborn, wanting to do everything myself. Yes, I know you hear the name *Martha*! (I *so* want to be like Mary!)

One day the sense of being overwhelmed became too heavy for me to bear. I was tired—trying to do it all in my own strength—and couldn't see how I could possibly give any more to my God-given dream, yet I felt very far from the hope of fulfilling anything purposeful in God's kingdom. There just wasn't enough of me to get everything done that was in my heart to do. Sound familiar? Well, God, who knows my heart, knows my mistakes, knows the things I'd done wrong, but also knows my potential, came and rescued me yet again, just when I was about to quit and walk away.

I had taken my girls to preschool and then went to a coffee shop, sat down, and started crying. Life was beginning to snowball into more than I was capable of handling. I just wanted to serve Jesus, and I really wasn't prepared for a lot of the demands that came with my new responsibilities of being the worship pastor.

I feared the call on my life would drive me crazy. I wanted to put it down, but I couldn't. So I argued, *"It's not my choice, Lord. I want to serve you, but you must take this call away from me because it's killing me. I'm trying to love my family, my church, my work; I'm trying, and I'm failing."* I pleaded with the Lord to take away the passionate desire in my heart to serve Him.

The people who worked in the coffee shop knew me really well, and I'm sure at that moment they thought I'd "lost the plot." Suddenly there was a knock on the window of the shop beside me. I looked up and saw my dear friend Melinda Hope, whom I hadn't seen in ages. She had come to our leadership college, and well, we fell in love with her and basically adopted her as our own. She had since married, and moved back to Tasmania (the little island that everyone forgets is part of Australia).

I was so happy to see Melinda. As she ran into the coffee shop, I felt excitement lift me as I asked, "What are you doing here?"

She said, "We've really felt God has been speaking to us about moving to Sydney, so Matt (her husband) has two job interviews lined up. Can we come around and tell you how they go?"

"Yes, of course!" I replied.

So they came to our house that afternoon and told us that Matt had been offered both of the jobs for which he'd interviewed, and he could choose whichever one he wanted. Then Mark said to Melinda, "We really need help in our home. It's nothing glamorous—we need help picking up the girls from school, cleaning, and having some meals ready. It's just that Darlene needs an extra set of hands."

Melinda started to cry and smile (which is a good kind of crying!) and said, "It's all I've ever wanted to do." Her heart has always been like this, no *pride,* willing to bless anyone in her path.

God is so faithful. That day I learned that when I am overwhelmed, He is faithful to His purpose, and on the journey, others find the way to fulfill their purpose too. There was not a lot of money to pay Melinda, yet she chose to bless us.

I needed an angel to help me with my daughters, because they are more precious to me than anything in the world. Trusting their care to someone is not up for grabs to the first person in the phone directory! I'm a steward of their lives, and God knew how I needed someone of excellent heart, like Melinda, to help me.

But here's the power of favor. As God met our immediate needs, He also was working in the lives of Mel and Matt. I watched God pick up those beautiful people and plant them in Sydney. (Of course, I often feel He sent them here *just for me*.) I've watched how they have been faithful to lay down everything for the Lord. I've watched them be obedient in season and out—when it suits and when it doesn't suit. I love them so much. I have seen the favor of God blessing their lives by their simply doing whatever needs to be done.

Matt now owns his own business, and God's blessing on them is amazing. They now have two little boys of their own, and their lives have gone from strength to strength. And it all started with their being willing and faithful servants.

It would have been naturally impossible to imagine Matt and Melinda going from where they were to where they are now. They've humbly sown into another person's vision, another person's life, and they've used their natural talents to release another person in ministry. They've proven that their faith is big enough to say, "Whatever it takes" to seek God's kingdom first, and now all the things have been added to them. Melinda is living proof that God rewards those who diligently seek Him with their whole heart.

Melinda and Matt united their purpose with ours. Unity demands a response from heaven. I think that's why the presence of God is poured out so magnificently over a body of people who choose to work together for a common goal. Harmony and agreement are not a natural state of today's world.

3. *Be part of a team, church, community.* A fully functioning community of believers covers one another; they make up for each other's weaknesses, and they help one another shine. When we understand God's purpose of working together, then being part of a corporate team of believers and worshipers is a very healthy and powerful place to be.

The Hillsong team enjoys great unity; we build each other up when we come together. That's one of the reasons why I think Hillsong Music has been allowed to have an impact in such a dramatic way. It is not from a core of people who just decided to make music together; it is from an amazing bunch of ordinary people who continually choose to say yes to whatever need presents itself. "Though one may be overpowered, two can defend themselves. A cord of three strands is not quickly broken" (Ecclesiastes 4:12).

The Word says that God "works out everything in conformity with the purpose of his will, in order that we, who were the first to hope in Christ, might be for the praise of his glory" (Ephesians 1:11–12). Second Thessalonians 1:11–12 says, "With this in mind, we constantly pray for you, that our God may count you worthy of his calling, and that by his power he may fulfill every good purpose of yours and every act prompted by your faith. We pray this so that the name of our Lord Jesus may be glorified in you, and you in him, according to the grace of our God and the Lord Jesus Christ."

There have been many times when I have questioned the possibility of my own dreams becoming a reality. But the Lord clearly spoke to me one day saying, *"Settle the issues once and for all: marriage, motherhood, and ministry. I've given them all to you."* With those words He breathed life into my calling. Once I knew the desire in my heart truly pleased Him, I no longer struggled with guilt and condemnation, which tries to strangle *so* many working women in today's society. Knowing I have His favor propels me to do whatever there is passion in my heart to do. His promise is in my spirit, and it holds me where I need to be.

The devil sometimes tries to tear my passion away from me by accusing me of unworthiness, or he mocks me in tired moments when I'm waiting on God for something, taunting, "You obeyed God, and God let you down." But I testify here that God has never ever let me down, and He won't let you down either. He is faithful to keep His promises. He is also good at stretching our faith to the eleventh hour. But He is faithful to fulfill in us the purpose of our calling.

I am fulfilled because I am walking with the Lord, in

His strength, not my own. When I am obedient to His leading, the power of His favor shines on my life and makes easy what otherwise would be too difficult to do.

I have learned to trust completely in God's purpose at work in my life—I trust His plan more than my own. I keep my mind full of His Word and my heart full of praise. And I pray this radical prayer, *Lord, whatever it takes, I want to serve you with my whole heart. Work in me so that your perfect will is performed through my life.*

Give God room to breathe on your dream.

I believe that God's favor shines on us when our passion radiates through our lives in pursuit of His purpose. Give God room to breathe on your dream. Dare to ask Him whether or not your passion is from Him. If He confirms it with His Word, lay aside your doubt and watch His favor bring it all to pass.

What you think is big and impossible is probably only the tip of the iceberg of what God wants to do through you. He will give you the strength to fulfill your dream. I challenge you to pick up the banner of determined passion that says, "Whatever it takes, I will follow the Lord."

Passion Is the Difference

When Mother Teresa was asked what sort of person could possibly tackle such an overwhelming problem as world poverty, she responded, "It's never a person who wants to save the world. They always become discouraged. But send me a contemplative. Send me someone who has a *deep heart for God,* and one day at a time, they serve."

"EVERY MAN DIES,

but NOT EVERY MAN TRULY LIVES..."

william wallace, "braveheart"

like stars in the universe

Twelve

LIKE STARS IN THE UNIVERSE

There is nothing more fulfilling than knowing God's purpose for your life and bearing fruit through His anointing on your work. Once God touches you with His power, that line of uncertainty over your calling is no longer an issue.

It is my prayer that the testimony of this book will be a reminder to you of God's awesome favor, His blessing, His power, His smile, His anointing—an amazing reality to live with as you love Him with your whole heart. His favor is the power to make your efforts to serve Him fruitful. His favor causes your endeavors to shine before the earth and thus fulfills the call Jesus laid before you, saying, "In the same way, let your light shine before men, that they may see your good deeds and praise your Father in heaven" (Matthew 5:16).

The word *hope* is significant to our earth's emotional climate, which is considered hopeless by so many. Does your life represent *hope*? Hope in an unchanging God . . . Hope in his Word and in His name? Hope suggests that there is a future, another chance, a hand to help you get up, strength for another day. . . . Hope goes beyond natural boundaries, and allows you to see into the land of possibility. You can see why the enemy would love to steal your vision of *hope* and cause hopelessness to overrule your current circumstance. Don't give him the privilege. Hang on! Hebrews 6:19 says, "We have this hope as an anchor for the soul, firm and secure."

Within my dream-seed from God is the desire to gather and embrace people from all walks of life and encourage them to trust their lives to the King and hope in the name of the Lord. The world is so full of people without hope, waking up afraid, falling asleep more terrified than the day before. Yet God's people live in a peace that passes all natural understanding or ability (see Philippians 4:7).

> *Arise, shine, for your light has come, and the glory of the* LORD *rises upon you. See, darkness covers the earth and thick darkness is over the peoples, but the* LORD *rises upon you and his glory appears over you.* (Isaiah 60:1–2)

The Word teaches that we're to follow the example of Christ (see Philippians 2:5). He walked a life of complete obedience. He stripped himself of all divine privileges that were available from His equality with God and submitted himself as a servant to humankind. Now that we, the church, are His body, we too must submit ourselves one to another in obedience to God's greater purpose of revealing His love to lost people, not only those in *the* world, but more specifically, those in *our* world.

We must yield our hearts to the task of building up those who are weak in order to fulfill the greater purpose that God has planned for this incredible time in history. Philippians 2:12–16 calls us to yield ourselves to the Lord, saying,

> *Therefore, my dear friends, as you have always obeyed—not only in my presence, but now much more in my absence—continue to work out your salvation with fear and trembling, for it is God who works in you to will and to act according to his good purpose.*
>
> *Do everything without complaining or arguing, so that you may become blameless and pure, children of God without fault in a crooked and depraved generation, in which you* shine like stars in the universe *as you hold out the word of life—in order that I may boast on the day of Christ that I did not run or labor for nothing.*

I totally *love* that picture—that we *should shine* not in our glory, but through holding out the Word of life! *Lovely.*

Verse 13 of this passage in *The Amplified Bible* says, "[Not in your own strength] for it is God Who is all the while effectually at work in you—energizing and creating in you the power *and desire*—both to will and to work for His good pleasure and satisfaction and delight." God promises to do the work in us and through us. All we need to do is submit our will to His, worship Him in truth for who He is, and walk with purpose toward that which He has predestined for us to do.

In our current society, people are so used to immediate gratification that waiting for God's perfect timing requires great strength of character. *Patience* has sadly become one of the words that is very unpopular in today's instant culture. But God is a *builder* of lives, and the finest buildings—the ones that remain—take time. The foundations have to be strong and certain to withhold the weathering that time and life bring on its journey.

God takes average lives and causes them to flourish and become significant. It will often seem easier to try to do good works in our own flesh and in our own strength to make our dreams happen quickly, but the Bible is full of tragic stories of people who knew they had a dream from God, but nearly sabotaged the plan because they weren't willing to wait on God. Sarah knew that God said she would have a baby, but in her eagerness to "help God," she sent her handmaiden to Abraham to bear a son for her (see Genesis 16:1–6).

Rebekah knew that Jacob was to inherit his brother's birthright, but instead of letting God work it out, she devised a deception to hurry the process along, and suffered many years while her beloved Jacob was in exile (Genesis 27:5–29, 41–45). Whenever God's people tried to make their heart's desire a reality by their own power, they paid a severe price that affected following generations.

We were never called to live this supernatural life from natural means. We were created to live it in the power of the Holy Spirit. We have been wired to depend totally on God to achieve His dream-seed. " 'Not by might nor by power, but by my Spirit,' says the LORD Almighty" (Zechariah 4:6).

Many believers are hesitant to yield their will to God because they only see the price of dying to self instead of the great reward that awaits them if they do what God tells them to do, and dying to self *hurts*!

God may only be asking you to do a simple thing at first, such as volunteer your time for something that takes away from more exciting plans. He may ask you to give away something that means a great deal to you. He may even ask you to forgive someone whom you feel you cannot forgive. Whatever it is He wants from you, obedience always brings the greatest reward. He is not likely to assign to you the bigger dream until you prove faithful in the smaller things.

Quick obedience causes our faces to radiate with peace. If we trust God, submitting and yielding to His authority, we will see our dream become a reality much faster.

It's easy to submit to someone if you agree with him or her, but then it isn't really submission. Abraham submitted to the Lord even when he didn't agree. Because Abraham submitted his own will to the Lord's, God told him, "I will surely bless you and make your descendants as numerous as the stars in the sky and as the sand on the seashore. Your descendants will take possession of the cities of their enemies, and through your offspring all nations on earth will be blessed, because you have obeyed me" (Genesis 22:17–18). All the nations of the earth are *blessed* because one man yielded himself to God. God didn't say it was because of Abraham's talent or giftedness, but blessing came to all nations because of his *obedience.*

A submitted heart releases God's redeeming favor into our situations and into the lives of others. God even gives us the strength, will, and desire to obey His Word. He makes obedience easy for those who submit their will to His. Once we step out to obey, God does the work in us for His own pleasure, satisfaction, and delight.

> *So be careful to do what the* LORD *your God has commanded you; do not turn aside to the right or to the left. Walk in all the way that the* LORD *your God has commanded you, so that you may live and prosper and prolong your days in the land that you will possess.* (Deuteronomy 5:32–33)

If we walk in obedience to what God tells us, we will prosper and live long, fulfilling lives. If we feel like standing still when we hear Him call to us, perhaps we should review our list of reasons why we call Him Lord.

We revere the Lord (fear Him) because of who He is: He is our best friend, our comforter, and our ever-present companion. He's also the Creator of the universe, He is the Alpha and Omega, the beginning and the end, the first and the last. He is the author of eternal salvation, He is our healer, He is our provider. He is the light of the world, the morning star, the Messiah, our Saviour. He cannot be contained within the English language or within the span of creation. He is Lord.

If we walk in obedience to what God tells us, we will prosper and live long, fulfilling lives.

Malachi 3:16–18 says,

> *Then those who feared the LORD talked with each other, and the LORD listened and heard. A scroll of remembrance was written in His presence concerning those who feared the LORD and honored his name.*
>
> *"They will be mine," says the LORD Almighty, "in the day when I make up my treasured possession. I will spare them, just as in compassion a man spares his son who serves*

him. And you will again see the distinction between the righteous and the wicked, between those who serve God and those who do not."

Be Salt and Light!

We, God's children, are called to be salt and light on the earth by offering the word of life to all people living in the dark hopelessness of the world (see Philippians 2:15–16). Some believers are afraid they will lose their friends if they speak up and testify of God's work in their lives. But they will lose them for eternity if they don't demonstrate God's love for them now. Jesus said,

Blessed are you when people insult you, persecute you and falsely say all kinds of evil against you because of me. Rejoice and be glad, because great is your reward in heaven, for in the same way they persecuted the prophets who were before you.

You are the salt of the earth. But if the salt loses its saltiness, how can it be made salty again? It is no longer good for anything, except to be thrown out and trampled by men.

You are the light of the world. A city on a hill cannot be hidden. Neither do people light a lamp and put it under a bowl. Instead they put it on its stand, and it gives light to everyone in the house. In the same way, let your light shine

before men, that they may see your good deeds and praise your Father in heaven. (Matthew 5:11–16)

If we try to hide God's presence or never speak of our intimate relationship with Him, how will unbelievers know what it's like to enjoy a living relationship with Christ? Without our testimony of God's grace, favor in our lives may seem like the result of following certain rules. A lot of religions already offer that, but Christianity is not a religion. It's not about our church attendance or religious duties. Our fulfillment is the result of a living relationship with the living God.

God's purpose for some of us may seem small; perhaps He will call us to help only a few people during the entire span of our lives. His purpose for others may be huge; He may have planted a dream-seed in one of us that will help millions of other people to know Him. Regardless of the size of the dream He plants within us, we enjoy the same sense of fulfillment when His dream for us is realized.

Fulfillment is not dependent on the size of our dream, but on understanding the size of God's investment in us to see that dream fulfilled. Satisfaction comes when we are aware of His favor on our steps of faith, when we see His hand multiply our efforts and watch the natural become the supernatural.

God's Word says, "One generation will commend your works to another; they will tell of your mighty acts. They will speak of the glorious splendor of your majesty, and I will meditate on your wonderful works" (Psalm 145:4–5). It also says, "Oh, that their hearts would be inclined to fear me and keep all my commands always, so that it might go well with them and their children forever!" (Deuteronomy 5:29). What a wonderful promise to know that obedience to the Lord will bless our children forever!

My own grandparents (affectionately known as Nan and Pop) have walked with the Lord for many, many years. I will never take for granted their years of sacrifice, love, and devotion to their Savior, their prayers and diligence when it comes to the house of God, and their total adoration when it comes to their family, for it has been an integral part of my walk with the Lord. We are a part of the inheritance God so graciously promises to those who love Him.

When we give thanks and praise God
for what He has done for us,
His favor is multiplied to us.

When we give thanks and praise God for what He has done for us, His favor is multiplied to us. When Jesus gave thanks for the few loaves of bread that had been given to

Him, God blessed the loaves and fed thousands with it (see Matthew 14:15–21).

Jesus met ten lepers who called for healing, and He cleansed all of them of their disease.

> *And one of them, when he saw that he was healed, turned back, and with a loud voice glorified God, and fell down on his face at his feet, giving him thanks: and he was a Samaritan.*
>
> *And Jesus answering said, "Were there not ten cleansed? But where are the nine? There are not found that returned to give glory to God, save this stranger." And he said unto him, "Arise, go thy way: thy faith hath made thee whole"* (Luke 17:15–19 KJV).

The word *whole* in this passage is from the Greek word *sozo*, which is defined in *Strong's Concordance* as "deliver, protect, heal, preserve, save and do well." This implies that the leper who returned with thankfulness was made whole in every area of his life, beyond the disease from which he had been delivered.

I could fill pages with all that we are thankful for. But most of all, I am thankful for the grace and favor of God, His heavenly kiss—so undeserved, but so needed. Start where you are. Delight God's heart by serving Him. Do well with whatever is in your hand today, and you *will* sense God's smile as you desire to love Him above all. Be blessed, dear friend, as you allow yourself to be changed by the almighty hand of our loving God.

As Martin Luther King said in one of the last sermons he gave before his death, "You don't have to have a college degree to serve. You don't have to make your subject and your verb agree to serve. You don't have to know about Plato and Aristotle to serve. You don't have to know Einstein's theory of relativity to serve. You only need a heart full of grace. A soul generated by love. And you can be that servant."

Forever,

Darlene Zschech

My prayer for you, above all else, is that you come into divine relationship with the author of love himself, Jesus Christ. Allow His perfect love to invade your life and take your breath away.

We were never created or designed

to live life on our own

without relationship with Jesus Christ.

We were never created or designed to live life on our own without relationship with Jesus Christ. Jesus said, " 'I am the way, the truth, and the life. No one comes to the Father except through me' " (John 14:6 NKJV). If you would like to surrender your life to God through faith in Jesus Christ, then I would like to encourage you, with all that I am, to pray the following prayer today.

Salvation Prayer

Dear Lord Jesus,

Today I confess my need of you. Thank you for dying on the cross so that I may have life.

Thank you for forgiving me of my sin.

Thank you for loving me, and thank you for the privilege of loving you.

Please give me the strength to follow hard after you, with all my heart and soul.

I commit my life into your hands.

I will love you forever.

Amen.

If you have prayed this prayer for the first time or have surrendered your life to Christ anew, please contact us at Hillsong Church, *hillsong@hillsong.com.*

Live to delight the ♡ of God.

I love you,

Darlene

As God's fellow workers we urge you not *to* receive God's grace *in* vain. For he says, "In *the* time *of* my favor I heard you, *and in the* day *of* salvation I helped you."

I tell you, now is *the* time *of* God's favor, now is *the* day *of* salvation.

2 corinthians 6: 1-2

the kiss of heaven

I'M WALKING A NEW WALK

I'LL NEVER BE THE SAME AGAIN

DANCING A NEW DANCE

IN YOUR HOLY SPIRIT RAIN

YOUR BREATH OF LIFE HAS OVERWHELMED ME

AND SET MY SPIRIT FREE

I'M LIVING A NEW LIFE

UNDERNEATH YOUR MORNING STAR

RUNNING A NEW RACE

IN THE SHADOW OF YOUR LOVE

YOUR LOVE IS IMMEASURABLE

TOO DEEP TO COMPREHEND

MY JESUS, DREAM-MAKER

MY JESUS, LIFE-GIVER

I'M LIVING UNDER THE KISS OF HEAVEN

AND I'LL NEVER EVER BE THE SAME AGAIN

I'M SINGING A NEW SONG

IN THE PRESENCE OF THE KING

GIVING YOU MY HEART

THAT IS ALL THAT I CAN BRING

YOU LIT A FIRE INSIDE OF ME
THAT I THOUGHT WOULD NEVER BURN AGAIN
MY JESUS, I SURRENDER
MY JESUS, YOURS FOREVER
I'M LIVING IN THE EMBRACE OF HEAVEN
AND I'LL NEVER EVER BE THE SAME AGAIN
I THANK YOU, MY FATHER
FOR ALL YOU'VE DONE AND ALL YOU ARE GOING TO DO
MY PAST BEHIND ME AND YOU BEFORE ME
I PRESS ON FOR MORE

*"Be strong and courageous and get to work.
Don't be frightened by the size of the task, for the
Lord my God is with you; he will not forsake you.
He will see to it that everything is finished correctly"*
(1 Chronicles 28:20 TLB).

DARLENE ZSCHECH has been part of the Hillsong Church praise team since 1986, has led the Worship and Creative Arts Department since 1996, and is co-producer of Hillsong Music Australia's highly successful albums. While she's always writing new praise and worship songs, she's best known for "Shout to the Lord," sung around the world. Darlene and her husband, Mark, and their daughters make their home in Sydney, Australia.

Mercy Ministries

A U S T R A L I A

A few years ago, during a trip to the USA, Mark and I were introduced to Nancy Alcorn, the founder of Mercy Ministries. On that day, God breathed life into a long-time dream that we'd held carefully in our hearts...
to be involved in seeing broken lives restored, and lovingly put back together by the immeasurable power of our awesome Lord.

I encourage you to join with us in supporting this valuable work.

Mark & Darlene Zschech

Mercy Ministries provides support for young women struggling with eating disorders, drug & alcohol abuse and unplanned pregnancy. Care is given absolutely free of charge, and includes practical training in areas such as budgeting, nutrition and fitness, as well as specific counselling for each girl's needs. Together, we see these beautiful young women emerge confident, and full of hope for the future.

MERCY MINISTRIES AUSTRALIA, PH: 1800 011 537, PO BOX 1537
CASTLE HILL, NSW 1765, AUSTRALIA, WWW.MERCYMINISTRIES.COM.AU

MERCY MINISTRIES OF AMERICA, PH: (615) 831 6987, PO BOX 111060
NASHVILLE, TN 37222-1060 USA, WWW.MERCYMINISTRIES.COM

*Everyone wants the best for their children… that's why I
sponsor two girls with Compassion. Our two sponsored girls
receive health care, food, education and importantly… hear
the Gospel through their local church. It's a joy to receive
their letters and be involved in their lives.*

*By sponsoring a child through Compassion you really will
make a difference – to the child and to the community. Just
think of the difference we can make if we all sponsor a child.*

Darlene Zschech

TO FIND OUT MORE ABOUT HOW YOU CAN
SPONSOR A CHILD, PLEASE CONTACT
COMPASSION TODAY.

PH: 1800 224 453 WWW.COMPASSIONAUST.COM.AU

darlene zschech
kiss of heaven

𝒯he songwriter behind the classics "Shout to the Lord" and "The Potter's Hand" reveals another side of her multi-faceted musical talent with her debut U.S. solo release, *Kiss of Heaven.* Springing from a platform of vertical expression, Darlene dives into a lyrical exploration of the more earthbound pursuits of our hearts and the idea of finding God's grace and love in reaching out toward one another.

Kiss of Heaven will introduce you to another side of Darlene that will boldly capture your imagination and musical senses while her overwhelming passion for worship and heart for the church continue to brightly shine through.

It's message and meaning are simple:

"It's just the love of my family, my adoration of my God, and my love of music. It's me. It's the things that are valuable to me."

—Darlene Zschech